YORK NOTES

General Editors: Professor A.N. Jeffares (*University of Stirling*) & Professor Suheil Bushrui (*American University of Beirut*)

T.S. Eliot

MURDER IN THE CATHEDRAL

Notes by Tony Bareham

MA (OXFORD) D PHIL (COLERAINE)
Senior Lecturer in English,
The New University of Ulster

D1136605

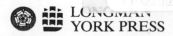

LONGMAN
YORK PRESS

Extracts from *Murder in the Cathedral* by T.S. Eliot are
reprinted by kind permission of Faber and Faber Ltd, London;
and in the U.S.A. by kind permission of Harcourt Brace Jovanovich, Inc.,
New York, copyright 1935 by Harcourt Brace Jovanovich, Inc.,
renewed 1963 by T.S. Eliot.

YORK PRESS
Immeuble Esseily, Place Riad Solh, Beirut.

LONGMAN GROUP LIMITED
Longman House, Burnt Mill, Harlow,
Essex CM20 2JE, England
and Associated Companies throughout the World.

© Librairie du Liban 1981

First published 1981
Reprinted 1983 and 1986
ISBN 0 582 78217 1

Produced by Longman Group (FE) Ltd
Printed in Hong Kong

Contents

Part 1

Introduction

Life of T.S. Eliot

Thomas Stearns Eliot was born in Saint Louis, Missouri, in 1888. He graduated from Harvard in 1910, then studied in Paris, in Germany, and at Merton College, Oxford. This diverse and distinguished career as a scholar is reflected in the close-packed intellectual content of Eliot's poetry and plays, in the depth of his background knowledge of such subjects as philosophy and religion, and in the range and compass of his interests.

Eliot returned to America in 1912, but by 1914 he was back in Europe, settling finally in England. He taught briefly at Highgate School in London; from 1919 to 1922 he was a bank clerk; and subsequently he became literary editor for the publishers Faber and Faber. He was, meanwhile, writing busily. *Prufrock and Other Observations* appeared in 1917, and *Poems* in 1919.

In 1922 Eliot was appointed editor of *The Criterion*, which became a highly influential critical review; in the first issue appeared his poem *The Waste Land*, which was subsequently hailed by many critics as a cornerstone of the modern English poetic movement. *The Waste Land* expresses despair, and disgust at the triviality of modern life; these sentiments helped to make the poem seem even more urgent to a generation suffering the after-effects of the First World War.

Eliot was, however, undergoing a steady change towards Christianity, driven by his private spiritual convictions and by his belief in the moral purpose of literature, the value of tradition to the artist, and the role of discipline in creative writing.

He once described himself as 'classicist in literature, royalist in politics, and anglo-catholic in religion'. It should be no surprise, therefore, that his poetry became increasingly coloured by religious themes and images, or that, in 1928, he became a British subject.

During the 1920s Eliot's reputation as a poet was augmented by his growing stature as a critic. He favoured particularly the earlier periods of English literature—the Metaphysical poets of the seventeenth century, and the Elizabethan contemporaries of Shakespeare. He helped to bring much of this highly intellectual poetry back into fashion.

In the next decade he turned to drama. *Murder in the Cathedral* (1935) was his first full-length play, but it had been preceded by at least two experiments in dramatic form—*Sweeney Agonistes* (1932) and *The Rock* (1934), a religious pageant. In 1935 he was invited to write a play for the Canterbury Festival, and *Murder in The Cathedral* was the result. Eliot wrote four more plays: *The Family Reunion* (1939), *The Cocktail Party* (1949), *The Confidential Clerk* (1953), and *The Elder Statesman* (1958). In addition *Murder in the Cathedral* was made into a film in 1951.

All his dramas are written in verse; Eliot was among the leaders of the movement to reintroduce verse into modern English drama. *Murder in the Cathedral* is felt by many critics to be his most successful attempt at combining the needs of poetry with those of live drama.

Eliot's other principal works include *Four Quartets* (1943), usually regarded as containing his finest poetry, and *On Poetry and Poets* (1957), which expresses many of his closely considered opinions on literature. *Old Possum's Book of Practical Cats* (1939), which he wrote for children, is certainly his most delightful and approachable poetry, the rare relaxation of a writer usually regarded as highly complicated and 'difficult'.

T.S. Eliot died in 1965, widely respected and admired as one of the most formative and influential poets of this century.

Background to the play

The turmoil which preceded Henry II

When England was invaded and conquered by King William of Normandy in the year 1066, a new line of foreign kings imposed themselves on the English people. As with all conquests followed by occupations there was political tension, and the ruling household was divided among itself in its claims to the new kingdom. William the Conqueror was followed by his third son, William Rufus, who was shot (probably deliberately) while hunting. Next to reign was Henry I, Rufus's younger brother.

It is always urgent for a newly established monarch to make sure he has sons to follow him in power. Henry had no legitimate sons, and since no woman had ever before occupied the English throne, when he died in 1135 his daughter Matilda's claim to the throne was disputed by her cousin Stephen. Murder, torture, kidnapping and extortion were rife as they fought for control of the country, and as individual barons seized the opportunity to create private armies. The Chorus in *Murder in the Cathedral* refers to this period in its opening speech:

King rules or barons rule;
We have suffered various oppression.

Henry II (1133–1189)

England needed a strong king to restore order after this civil war. Henry II, grandson of Henry I, was such a man. He was forthright, determined, and often, by modern standards, downright ruthless. Because of the unfortunate events surrounding Becket's death it is easy to see the King as the villain of the story. The truth is more complex. In his attempt to restore order Henry sought the aid of strong and able men such as Becket, who was an administrator of exceptional ability. Henry loaded him with power, and then, just as a state of order seemed to have been reached, Becket began to oppose the King. Henry was just the kind of person to be outraged at what he saw as a breach of trust by the friend to whom he had given everything.

Thomas Becket (1118–1170)

Becket was not a nobleman by birth; he was the son of a London merchant, though he found this no obstacle to achieving the highest honours in the kingdom. Recognised from his youth as a scholar, Becket was also a great lover of life; he was an expert on the dance floor, in the jousting field and at the hunt.

He was trained as a lawyer, and attracted the attention of Theobald, the Archbishop of Canterbury, who offered him employment. Becket rose quickly from being a secretary to the position of archdeacon—a position of considerable trust for a man of thirty-six. By 1156 his talents had come to the notice of the King. So highly did he rate Becket's ability that he made him Chancellor of England. Henry is said to have been the only person Becket ever really loved. As Chancellor Becket showed incorruptible honesty and inexhaustible energy. Despite the suggestion of the Knights in Eliot's play, Becket also seems to have been a man who could not be tempted or corrupted by the life of the court. He led a chaste and seemly life—by no means a common thing at this time.

In 1162 King Henry made Becket Archbishop of Canterbury. Becket warned the King that if he accepted the office he would serve the Church before the State should a clash of interests arise. He insisted on resigning as Chancellor before accepting the Archbishopric.

Such clashes of interest soon occurred. Within two years of his appointment as Archbishop of Canterbury relationships deteriorated; the King sought to imprison Becket, who fled across the sea to Flanders and on several occasions appealed to the Pope to protect him from Henry's attempts to make him return to England. A shaky peace was made in July 1170, but numerous causes of quarrel remained between these two proud and stubborn men, each of whom retained fixed ideas of the place of Church and State in the government of the kingdom.

At Christmas 1170 Becket determined to return to Canterbury, arriving in time to preach his Christmas sermon (as in Eliot's play). He was then murdered in his own cathedral on 29 January.

Political background: the Constitutions of Clarendon

In the reign of King Stephen the Church had, rightly or wrongly, taken into its own hands the duty of judging and punishing clergymen who committed crimes. Since there were legal limitations on the punishments which Church courts could inflict this meant that sentences given to clergymen and to a layman for the same offence could be drastically different. A layman committing murder, for instance, could be executed. But Church courts could not impose the death sentence, so a cleric who committed the same crime got off much more lightly if tried in a Church court.

Henry II wished to bring all justice under the control of the secular authority. The Church opposed him since it felt a loss of power would be involved, and because it argued that its loyalty was as much to the Pope in Rome as to the King of England. The King drew up a document which, in sixteen points or 'constitutions', sought to define the relationship between the power of the King (the secular power), and that of the Church (the ecclesiastical power). This document was presented for the Church's consideration at Clarendon in 1164 and Becket, in the name of the Church to whose highest office Henry had appointed him, opposed it. His opposition infuriated the King. Charges, probably false, were made that Becket had mal-administered his accounts when he was Chancellor. This enabled the King to threaten Becket without the Church having any excuse for interference. Seeing his danger, Becket fled to Flanders.

The coronation

Henry wished to establish the claim of his sons to follow him in power. He decided to arrange that his son, Prince Henry, should be presented to the people and formally crowned while he himself was still alive. It was customary for the coronation to be performed by the Archbishop of Canterbury. But Henry's Archbishop was by now living in fear of his life in France.

The King persuaded the Archbishop of York, with the Bishops of London and Salisbury, to perform the ceremony. Becket immediately appealed to the Pope against this breach of his authority. The Pope attempted a reconciliation, though he was clearly on Becket's side, as was the King of France, with whom Becket had sought refuge. An uneasy truce between King and Archbishop was called at Montmirail in France in July 1170. Becket still refused to make any firm promise to accept the Constitutions of Clarendon, and the King did not give him the formal kiss of peace (the symbolic gesture indicating complete royal forgiveness). Eliot refers to this:

FIRST PRIEST
. . . is it war or peace?
MESSENGER
Peace, but not the kiss of peace;
A patched-up affair . . . (p.27)

Clearly the danger to Becket was by no means over.

The murder

Matters came to a head when Henry learned that Becket had asked the Pope to excommunicate the Archbishop of York and the Bishops of London and Salisbury for their part in the coronation of Prince Henry, a most serious interference by the clergy in secular affairs. On hearing the news, Henry made an angry exclamation, to the effect of, 'What slothful wretches I have brought up in my kingdom, who have no more loyalty to their king than to suffer him to be so disgracefully mocked by this low-born cleric!' Another version has it that the King's words were, 'Will no man rid me of this turbulent priest?' Some of those who heard his expression of anger took it as an invitation to act. Reginald Fitz Urse, Hugh de Morville, William de Traci and Richard Brito went to Canterbury, where they arrived just before Christmas, only a few days after Becket returned from exile, and confronted Becket. The Archbishop, refusing the protection of the terrified monks, and forbidding the closure of the cathedral doors against the knights, faced them bravely. 'Far be it from me to make a castle of the Church of God', he is reported to have said. The knights then struck him down and murdered him on a flight of steps within the cathedral.

Their action gave to the English Church its most potent martyr. Within a few years of his death the tomb of Becket (who was canonised in 1173) was the resort of pilgrims from all over Europe. Miraculous cures were supposed to be effected there. The pilgrims in Geoffrey Chaucer's poem *The Canterbury Tales* (c.1386) are on their way to Becket's shrine. The tomb itself was destroyed at the time of the Reformation, about 1540.

A note on the text

The first edition of *Murder in the Cathedral* was the version acted at the Canterbury Festival in 1935. The different needs of the professional theatre where the play was subsequently staged resulted in some changes to the text. The detail of these changes is given in E. Martin Browne's book *The Making of T.S. Eliot's Plays* (see Part 5, Suggestions for further reading).

Browne, who produced the play, explains that he wished the Fourth Knight to remain rather aloof from the bullying of the other three; 'It seemed to me that, dramatically, this figure should throughout be a figure of mystery, who while not participating in the violence could be felt as the influence behind it.'

The final version is that of *Collected Plays*, Faber and Faber, London, 1962. Virtually all subsequent editions have been based on this version.

For these notes the edition of 1968 (1976 reprint) has been used. Because there are numerous editions of the play, reference is given throughout to both page and line numbers. It is suggested that students whose text does not correspond to that used here should insert line numbers into their copies, for ease of following detailed references.

Part 2

Summaries
of MURDER IN THE CATHEDRAL

A general summary

Part I of *Murder in the Cathedral* describes the return of Becket from exile in France. The women of the Chorus express their anxiety; the seasons have passed by, and they have contrived somehow to eke out a living. Now, at this Christmastide, they fear some unknown disruption.

A Messenger informs the Priests that Becket will soon be with them. He has not, however, been properly reconciled with King Henry. While the Priests are hopeful of the outcome, the Chorus again expresses its doubts.

Soon after his arrival, Becket is subjected to four temptations urging him to yield to Henry, or to his own instinct for martyrdom. The Chorus is bewildered, but Becket is now sure that he can accept God's will, even if this means martyrdom.

The Interlude, Becket's sermon, shows how the birth and crucifixion of Christ are parts of the same Christian mystery, of which all other martyrdoms for the Faith are a part. Becket warns that Canterbury may soon have another martyr: himself.

At the beginning of Part II the Chorus and Priests make us aware that four days have passed. The Knights appear, insisting on an interview with Becket, whom they accuse of treason, and of ingratitude to the King. They repeat Henry's command that Becket should leave England, but the Archbishop refuses.

The Chorus senses death in the air, and laments its inability to help Thomas. The Priests attempt to bustle him away from danger, but he forbids them to bar the doors. The Knights burst in and Becket is murdered, while the Chorus begs for release from the foulness of a world where such deeds occur.

The Knights attempt to give an explanation of their actions to the audience. When they depart, the Priests and the Chorus mourn Becket, deplore the desolate fate of his murderers, and prophesy a new glory for Thomas and for the Church. The play ends with a prayer for mercy by the members of the Chorus as they recognise their sin and weakness, and the sanctity of the newly created martyr.

Detailed summaries

Murder in the Cathedral is not constructed in acts and scenes in the conventional modern manner. The action is divided into two parts, divided by an interlude. This structure is discussed in detail on pp.43–6 below. *For study purposes only* it is convenient to subdivide the text as indicated in these notes.

Part I: Chorus, lines 1–50 (pages 11–13)

The Chorus of poor women of Canterbury is drawn to the shelter of the Cathedral by feelings of inexplicable fear, sensing that some momentous act is about to take place.

It is seven years since Thomas, the Archbishop of Canterbury, left his people to go into exile. Life has gone its normal way, for better or worse. Now, in this bitter winter season, they sense danger, and do not want the Archbishop to return, lest the pattern of their lives should be disturbed.

NOTES AND GLOSSARY:

Chorus: Eliot has taken the device of the Chorus from Greek drama. This is further discussed on pp.33–5. These poor women of Canterbury are not meant to be 'characters' in the usual dramatic sense; they are representatives of common humanity, everywhere and in all places

cathedral: in times past, when danger threatened, people fled to the nearest church, which because it was dedicated to God, was regarded as sacred ground within which nobody could be harmed. This was called 'taking sanctuary'. Hence the note of fear, of awareness of impending disaster, is present from the very beginning of the play

poor women: by making his Chorus comprise these lowly women Eliot gives a solid core of humanity to his rather abstract play

presage: warning

our eyes are compelled to witness: though they do not yet know what will occur, the Chorus members unconsciously feel that forthcoming events will compel them to be spectators. But the Greek word for 'witness' is *martyr*; hence Eliot is able to suggest the closeness of the relationship between the Chorus and the hero of the play

golden October . . . sombre November: the play extensively uses imagery of the passing seasons. Here Eliot indicates the passage of time and the continuing cycle of nature by the use of colourful words which suggested the fading of sunlight, the plunging of the year into winter darkness, and a consequent sense of imminent danger

brown sharp points of death: this builds up a picture of the English winter, cold and dark. Small areas of land rise out of the floods, while jagged sheets of rain descend. But the 'sharp points' also suggest the swords which will later kill Becket

The New Year waits: the Chorus creates a sense of expectancy; what is it—and the very season itself—waiting for? Usually New Year is a time of new beginnings, of optimism

the coming: Christmas is usually associated with the coming of Christ, but the atmosphere of the Chorus suggests something much darker

stretched out his hand to the fire: although this continues the imagery of ordinary life—'apples were gathered', 'the labourer kicks off a muddy boot'—it has other suggestions. In describing the events just before Christ's crucifixion the Bible (Mark 14: 54) says, 'And Peter followed him afar off, even into the palace of the high priest: and he sat with the servants, and warmed himself at the fire'

Eliot's phrase both here and at line 16 reminds us of the death of Christ just as 'the coming' has reminded us of his birth. This duality of outlook runs throughout the play with its emphasis upon martyrdom and life eternal

All Hallows: the feast of All Saints (Hallows) celebrates those who have died for Christ as martyrs, and sustains the idea of martyrdom built up by the Chorus

seven years: the seven-year period of Becket's exile, 1164-70

summer is over: this continues the imagery of the seasons, and suggests Becket's return may herald worse times to come

we are content if we are left alone: the Chorus, until very near the end of the play, desires not to be involved in the events taking place

in the hand of God, not in the hand of statesmen: this suggests that events in the divine pattern of things may be very different from those apparently caused by men themselves

happy December:	happy, as the season of Christ's birth
the litter of scorn:	the manger in a humble stable where Christ was born. The joy of birth is linked to the bitterness of death by suggesting the 'scorn' Christ suffered at the time of his crucifixion
there is no action:	the Chorus recognises its helplessness to do anything except watch and comment

Part I: Priests and Messenger, lines 51–110 (pages 13–16)

The Priests remind us again of Becket's seven-year absence. The interim has been a time of meetings, of agreements patched up and broken. Worldly power, argues the Third Priest, can never bring stability.

A Messenger brings news of the Archbishop's imminent return. The Messenger can give no assurance that Becket and Henry are reconciled. Becket still has the love of the people, who have flocked to welcome him, but with the King he has only an uneasy truce, to which neither has given wholehearted assent. The Messenger suggests that Becket knows that his life may be drawing to a violent close.

NOTES AND GLOSSARY:

Archbishop ... Pope ... King ... French King: see 'Background to the play', pp.6–9 of these notes

temporal government: worldly, as opposed to spiritual, authority

duplicity: cheating

malversation: corrupt behaviour whilst in a position of trust

caprice: illogical whim

their friend, their Father in God: such descriptions of Becket underline his humanity and his closeness to the ordinary people, while never losing sight of his dignity and power as head of the English Church

without circumlocution: wasting no words

reunited: the Chorus's surprise is quite justified. Becket's quarrel with Henry had been very bitter and violent, and a reconciliation must have seemed most unlikely

the hammer and the anvil: that is, as between two immovable objects which can only damage each other when they clash

pride: the Second Priest recognises that Becket and Henry may be governed by pride

full assurance: this would mean complete peace between King and Archbishop, whereas his coming 'in the power of Rome', without Henry's goodwill, suggests the hostility of the State, and spells danger

incredulity: disbelief

in pride and sorrow: helps to suggest Becket's character and his actions later in the play. He is proud of his authority as Head of the Church, of his own integrity, and of the rightness of his cause. But he feels sorrow for the quarrel he is in, for the neglect of his people, and for the troubles his forthcoming death may bring upon them

Lining the road and throwing down their capes: as on Christ's last journey into Jerusalem: see the Bible, Mark 11:8, 'And many spread their garments in the way, and others cut down branches off the trees, and strawed them in the way'

deprived of its tail: so eager are the people to have a memorial of Becket, that they even pluck out the horse's hairs as souvenirs.

not the kiss of peace: the final token of royal forgiveness; without it no royal pardon was complete or binding

pretensions: claims, or points of view

this peace Is nothing like an end: not like the end of a quarrel nor the beginning of a peace. But the words have a deeper meaning too. The Messenger suggests that the actions now about to take place will still be felt centuries later. The martyrdom of Becket was to prove him right

My Lord . . . I leave you . . . : very close to the words Becket is reported to have addressed to Henry at their last parting in real life. Later these words are used by the Fourth Knight, perversely, to argue that Becket willed his own death (see Part II, p.89, ll.559–62)

prognostic: omen

Part I: Chorus and Priests, lines 111–205 (pages 16–21)

The First Priest is alarmed because he knows Becket's pride. He has always been a lonely figure, despising authority from temporal sources and admitting only the mastery which comes from God. Such pride, clashing with that of the King, spells danger.

The Second Priest is more hopeful; at least the Archbishop has come home. The people and clerics of Canterbury will now have a leader. The Chorus, however, begs Becket to return to France, fearing he brings with him death and disruption. Such cowardice earns the reproof of the Second Priest, who urges the Chorus to put on a welcoming face for Thomas.

NOTES AND GLOSSARY:

sudden prosperity: Becket rose to power with extraordinary speed

temporal devolution: handed down from a purely worldly as opposed to an ecclesiastical source

we can lean on a rock: the Priest sees Becket as a fixed point of stability in a sea of troubles. An appropriate image since (i) Becket has just made the dangerous journey over the sea from France; (ii) Christ called St Peter the rock on which he would build his church, and Becket as Archbishop has a direct link with St Peter; (iii) before writing *Murder in the Cathedral* Eliot had been working on a religious pageant about the London churches which he called *The Rock*

I am the Archbishop's man: in medieval times everybody 'belonged' to some higher person in authority. The Priest thinks of his duty to the Archbishop in these dangerously feudal terms, whereas he should think of himself only as 'belonging' to Christ

the wheel: this complex image is used again later in the play (p.22, l.216). The Third Priest means, broadly, 'let events move forward, time cannot stand still'

Until the grinders cease: a phrase from the Bible, Ecclesiastes 13:3–4, a passage which predicts the coming of a time of sorrow

Here is no continuing city: see the Bible, Hebrews 13:14, a passage reminding us that the things of this world all pass away

stay: this has two meanings: (i) a support; (ii) a resting-place

doom: judgement; ruin

living and partly living: the members of the Chorus recognise that their lives have been limited and petty. They fear that the return of Becket may destroy their tenuous peace. The phrase also sums up their spiritual impoverishment

luxury: here, excess

licence: abuse of freedom

void: complete emptiness

to stand to the doom: this phrase means both to be prepared for, and to withstand

unaffrayed: old-fashioned spelling of 'unafraid'

craven: cowardly

apprehension: fear

Part I: Archbishop and Priests, lines 206-54 (pages 21-3)

The Archbishop returns. He reproves the Second Priest for scolding the Chorus. He has so far avoided his enemies, but predicts that they will soon swoop down on him. In the meantime he has another trial to undergo.

NOTES AND GLOSSARY:

exaltation: a state of intellectual excitement

action is suffering . . .: this is perhaps the most difficult speech in the play, containing an idea which is repeated several times. The Chorus wish Becket to go away, to avoid action. It will make no difference, however, for all suffering is a kind of action, and conversely, every act brings about some suffering, some experience

(i) agent; (ii) patient: (i) a person who acts; (ii) a person who endures without having taken action. In the original script Eliot wrote 'actor' for 'agent'. To the reader this would be clear, but in the theatre the word 'actor' was ambiguous and it had to be changed

both are fixed: repeats the idea of the inevitable relationship between action and suffering; both form parts of God's overall pattern for human life

subsist: have existence

wheel: this returns to the concept first suggested by the Third Priest at line 137. In medieval times the phases of human fortune were often depicted as though fixed to a wheel, with some men rising, some at the height of their fortune, and some, inevitably, tumbling off as the wheel plunged them downwards. Eliot also has the idea of time being *cyclic*, of all events taking place within a closed circle of time. This circle has a revolving rim, on which human actions are fixed, but the centre, the hub of the wheel, is the still point of eternity with God as its centre. Becket is pondering whether to take any action in his dealings with King Henry, or whether simply to let things take their course

a better climate: Becket has just returned from the sunny weather of France. This is probably also meant as a metaphor for 'used to better fortune than your present one'

And will try to leave them . . .: Becket hints that he knows events are going to interrupt his everyday business before he has time to untidy his room

York, London, Salisbury: the three who carried out the illegal coronation and whom Becket has asked the Pope to excommunicate

prevision: foreknowledge

Sandwich: the town on the south coast of England where Becket landed from France

Broc, Warenne . . . : Ranulf de Broc, master of Saltwood Castle in Kent, entertained the Knights both before and after the murder. The other names are those of men who the chronicles tell us were also pitted against Becket

John, the Dean of Salisbury: one of the few clerics who dared stand up for Becket when he returned

warning against treason: since Becket and the King were supposedly at peace after their last meeting it was an act of treason to oppose the Archbishop's presence in England

hawk: Eliot uses the image of a savage hunting-bird to create a picture of the bloodthirsty Knights waiting for their chance to swoop on Becket

the substance of our first act: 'act' has two meanings here: (i) 'action'; (ii) the act of a play. Becket says that his first action now he is back in England will be to do battle with 'shadows', by which he means the Tempters who are about to appear. Eliot also suggests that the rest of the first act of the play will contain only abstract ideas, not the physical deeds the audience may be expecting

heavier the interval than the consummation: the intervening time— 'interval'—of his life and of the play, will be more difficult for him—'heavier'—than the conclusion itself. Becket is aware that the temptations he is about to undergo will be more testing than the murder which is to follow later

all things prepare the event: everything plays its part in bringing about the inevitable conclusion

watch: a 'watch' is a religious vigil, a period in which a man voluntarily deprives himself of sleep in order to experience a spiritual insight. It also means a specific period of sentry duty. Both meanings are present here as Becket prepares for the arrival of the Tempters. There is a theatrical problem at this point, which the word 'watch' helps to solve. For nearly four hundred lines neither Chorus nor Priests have anything to say or do. Should they leave the stage? Their exit slows things down and is distressing. But they must be quite still if they remain during the Tempters scene. At the word 'watch' it is of course perfectly proper for them to kneel as though undergoing a vigil

Part I: Archbishop and Tempters, lines 255-599 (pages 25-43)

The Archbishop undergoes four temptations. Each represents an aspect of his past or future life. The First Tempter suggests that Becket might patch up his differences with the King, and recalls earlier, more enjoyable days. But Becket is no longer to be tempted by the life of physical appetites and bodily ease.

The Second Tempter suggests that Becket should regain the Chancellorship. The Chancellor has more real power than the King, and such power can be used for good. But Becket realises that, in order to regain this worldly power, he must give up his spiritual authority.

The Third Temper claims to speak for the ordinary English people who want Becket as their figurehead in a nationalist struggle against the foreigners who surround the King. Becket admits that he has been attracted by the idea of breaking the very authority he helped, as Chancellor, to make.

The Fourth Tempter takes him by surprise. He suggests that Becket should deliberately seek martyrdom. This will grant him the best kind of fame: 'fame after death'. Becket is shaken by this statement of his own most secret thoughts and anxieties. He does not see how he can avoid the issue, for if he acts he will be damned for worldly ambition, and if he seeks martyrdom for selfish glory he will be damned for spiritual pride.

NOTES AND GLOSSARY:

acrimony: bitterness

levity: lack of seriousness

gay Tom: this refers to Becket's enjoyment of worldly pastimes in his youth

shall we say the summer's over: this continues the Chorus's earlier image of the summer. From the Chorus we already know that it is over by this time. There can be no return to the 'good old days' when Becket was on good terms with Henry

viols: medieval stringed instruments of the violin family

fires devouring the winter season: this again uses imagery first employed by the Chorus. The Tempter suggests that the joys of worldly pleasures can 'warm away' troubles and difficulties

seasons that are past: literally, years gone by, but also implying that they are over and done with, that Becket has no desire to go back to them

spring has come in winter: unlike the Chorus, which sees everything growing dark, this Tempter uses seasonal imagery to try to make Becket believe that all can be well again if he will make up his quarrel with Henry

matches: defeats

sever the cord: images of time moving forward in a way which cannot be reversed, as in the severing of the umbilical cord, or a reptile growing into a new skin

wheel: another reference to the wheel of fortune and the eternal cycle of life on which human existence is fixed

I am your man: earlier (1.136), the Second Priest had said 'I am the Archbishop's man', pledging a medieval troth to his overlord. Now the Tempter offers his own services to Becket. There is a subtle irony here, for if we think of the Knights and the Tempters as being played by the same actors, we shall learn later that the First Knight was indeed Becket's 'man'—Reginald Fitz Urse owed feudal allegiance to the Archbishop

not in this train: Becket continues the imagery taken from medieval royal courts: the 'train' comprised the King's followers. He also means 'not in this train of thought'

follow your master: this seems to refer again to the suggestion above that this Tempter in his other role as Fitz Urse owes allegiance to Becket who is, therefore, his 'master'. Hence, 'follow my example and turn your back on this worldly life. Also, 'follow Christ'—the 'master' of all men

gait: pace, way of walking

higher vices: the First Tempter has offered the good things of the world. Having failed, he leaves Thomas to his pride and ambition, which he perversely chooses to represent as 'vices', or sins of a more serious kind than those he has mentioned

higher prices: that is, spiritual damnation

the impossible is still temptation: though it is impossible to 'put the clock back' and return to the old days of Becket's youthful life, it is tempting to try

Clarendon . . . : various places where meetings between Henry and Becket occurred

policy: ability in political dealings
a mistake: the Tempter argues that Becket should have held
                        on to his secular power when he took office as Arch-
                        bishop. Becket had, however, insisted on resigning
                        because he felt the duties of the Archbishop might
                        well be in direct opposition to those of the Chan-
                        cellor
reckon: believe: 'do not believe that worldly power is a
                        foolish thing'
the solid substance: his power as Chancellor
deceitful shadows: the vague idea of spiritual duty and glory
commands . . . rules: the Chancellor has real power, the King has only
                        the appearance of it
sentence: piece of wisdom
rule for the good of the better cause: the Tempter suggests that if Becket
                        regains his worldly power he can use it for his own
                        spiritual purposes
means: methods
certain submission: Becket will have to submit some of his religious
                        principles to the King's pleasure
perdition: damnation, utter loss
pretence: false claim
bravery: defiance
cabined: imprisoned
realmless ruler: broken of his power and shut up in prison, Becket
                        would be helpless and futile as a king with no king-
                        dom ('realm')
the old stag: an image from hunting, as though Becket is a help-
                        less deer, surrounded by the King's ferocious dogs.
                        He has already been likened to a victim around
                        whom the hawks are wheeling
decorum: propriety
bishops: York, London and Salisbury; see p.9
excommunication: withholding the rights and privileges of the Catholic
                        Church, specifically Communion. This is regarded
                        as the final and most terrible punishment the
                        Church could inflict
Constant curbing of petty privilege: as Chancellor, Becket had made the
                        barons give up their individual courts and private
                        laws
churls: common people
I who keep the keys: the keys of authority symbolising the keys of St
                        Peter, the first Pope, who keeps the keys of the gates
                        of heaven

delegate:	share power (or, depending on the part of speech Eliot intends, it can mean 'having been delegated')
sin soars sunward:	another hunting image. A hawk rises towards the sun in order to blind its prey. The King's falcons (hawks), being royal property, should have the right to soar higher than all others. But, says the Tempter, Becket is so proud that he seeks to be above even the King
but arrest disorder:	do no more than put a temporary stop to unruliness
country-keeping:	a double meaning: (i) staying in the country, rather than going up to court; (ii) being responsible for governing the country
it is our country:	the Third Tempter assumes the role of one of the Norman barons who felt that the land should belong to them rather than to the foreigners with whom the King surrounded himself. The kings of England at this time had extensive lands in France, whence they had originally come. Thus the King often spent more time in France than in England, which was resented by those barons who had chosen to make their residence in England
not undetermined:	not without reasons which can be logically deduced
dark:	vague, obscure
You only look to blind assertion . . . :	Becket has rejected the King and is foolishly insisting on his rights (assertion) with no help or support from outside
hungry sons:	like most medieval rulers, Henry had the problem of satisfying and curbing the demands of all his sons for land to rule over. His plan to have Prince Henry crowned was part of his desire to keep due order among his sons
coalition:	alliance
tyrranous jurisdiction:	Henry had sought to impose the power of the Crown upon the Church courts
which I helped to found:	as Chancellor Becket had been active in setting up courts for imposing central government
constellation:	star, that is, leader
field:	either hunting-field or battle-field
tilt-yard:	the arena where tournaments between knights were held
To make, then break:	Becket acknowledges the real temptation to destroy the very law and order which he created. This would be a demonstration of power and sweet revenge against the King

Samson in Gaza: the Bible, Judges 16:21-30, tells how Samson, blind and in captivity, destroyed his enemies the Philistines by pulling down the house in which they sat watching and mocking him. But in destroying his foes Samson also slew himself. Revenge such as the Third Tempter suggests would be just as self-destructive for Becket

precede expectation: arrive before expected

you know me but have never seen my face: this is the most dangerous temptation. The others are all external temptations, representing aspects of worldly power and ambition. The last temptation comes from within the most secret parts of Becket's mind. Hence in a way he 'knows' this tempter, but he has never dared face him before, so has not 'seen his face'

hooks have been baited: this refers to the other three temptations as though these had been juicy bits of bait to catch a fish

Wantonness: self-indulgence, as in Becket's earlier life at court

skein: a coil of thread or wool

Supreme, but for one: that is, the Devil. The Bible, Matthew 4:9, tells how, during his temptations in the wilderness, Christ was offered supremacy over all else if only he would acknowledge the Devil

glory after death: not, of course, the same thing as martyrdom. If Becket consciously acts so that he brings death upon his own head, and if he does this simply because he wants men to think well of him, this will be the greatest sin he can commit. It is to this that the Tempter is leading him

shade: ghost

supplication: prayer

further scorning: the Tempter explains this a few lines later at 'the shrine shall be pillaged' and 'when miracles cease'. He envisages the time when it will no longer be fashionable to visit the tombs of saints and martyrs. At the Reformation (c.1540) Becket's tomb, like most other elaborate monuments in English churches, was pillaged of its gold and precious ornaments

when men will not hate you: this foretells the later, modern, time when even a saint will be seen just as a man playing a part in history

execrate: curse

gulf: the Bible, Luke 16:19-31, tells the parable of Dives (the rich man) and Lazarus (the beggar) between whom in hell and in heaven is fixed an unbridgeable gulf, or space. The Tempter suggests that as a martyr Becket will be able to look down on his enemies as, after his sufferings here on earth, Lazarus was able to look down on Dives

palpable: recognisable, obvious

perdition: damnation

You know and do not know: the Fourth Tempter is so much a part of Becket that he even uses Thomas's own words (compare p.22, ll.209-17)

Part I: Chorus, Priests, Tempters, Becket, line 600-end of Part 1 (pages 43-8)

The women sense an atmosphere of evil, as though they can discern the presence of the Tempters. They consider the futility of everyday life and show their dismay at what they think is Becket's desire for the self-glory which will come with martyrdom. The Priests urge him to yield to the pressure of events.

The Chorus, Tempters and Priests express a sense of the dangers and brevity of life, and the Chorus describes the trials of everyday existence. Despair comes to the women, for if Becket destroys himself for selfish ends their last hope will be gone.

At last Becket can see his way clearly. The Fourth Tempter has shown him that his motives and his actions must both be right before the deed itself can be so. If he seeks martyrdom only for his own glory it will be sinful. But if it comes to him as God's will, without his acting to cause it, then it cannot be misconstrued.

He recognises that many men will think him mad or vain because he takes no action to avoid his death; but he gives himself up totally to the will of God—his spiritual struggle is over.

NOTES AND GLOSSARY:

parturition: the act of giving birth

The Catherine wheel, the pantomime cat . . .: examples of things which seem attractive initially, but which lose their charm as we grow out of them. The list is intended to be slightly ridiculous or trivial, to symbolise the triviality of all human ambition

intractable: unmanageable

extortion: obtaining something by illegal force

destitution: extreme poverty

puss-purr; palm-pat: words made up by Eliot to conjure up the sounds of the beasts he is describing. By making them alliterative—that is, by making the first letters of all the words 'chime' with each other—he strengthens the sense of the sounds

square hyena: presumably 'square' because Eliot thinks of it as very solid and substantial. All these beasts are meant to elicit a sense of fear and horror

---

Interlude

Becket, now resolved in his mind about his future actions, preaches his Christmas sermon. His text uses the words spoken to the shepherds by the angels on the first Christmas night, reminding the audience of the birth of Christ. But Mass is a celebration principally of the Last Supper, recalling the crucifixion of Christ. Hence the celebrations at Christmas imply both birth and death; Christians both mourn and rejoice at this time.

The angels promised peace in their Christmas message, but Christ promised his disciples peace 'not as this world gives'. These disciples were forced to suffer for Christ in carrying his message far and wide. Some were made martyrs in the cause. On the very day after Christmas St Stephen became the first of the martyrs.

Martyrdom itself is cause for both weeping and rejoicing. It is a mystery sent from God, never merely an accident, nor a conscious act of human will. The true martyr gives his life and his will over completely to God, and no longer has any desires of his own.

Becket reminds his congregation that Canterbury already has one martyr—Archbishop Elphege—and says that it may soon have another —himself.

NOTES AND GLOSSARY:

Mass: strictly the celebration of the Lord's supper, then more generally, any of the major Christian festivals, as in Christ-mas. Hence, the Archbishop's sermon on this day re-enacts 'the Passion and Death of Our Lord' and at the same time is a 'celebration of His birth'

oblation: sacred offering

Beloved: the customary form of address by the priest to his congregation during the sermon

Peace I leave with you: from the Bible, John 14:27; Christ's own words to his disciples, spoken not long before he was crucified

His first martyr:	the martyrdom of St Stephen, which is celebrated on the day after Christmas, is described in Acts 6 and 7, especially 7:56–60
figure:	symbol
Elphege:	Elphege or Aelfeah, Archbishop of Canterbury AD1006–12. He was murdered by the Danes for refusing to pay ransom to them

---

Part II: Chorus and Priests, lines 1–62 (pages 57–61)

The Chorus gives expression to a feeling of darkness and bitterness, despite this being the season of Christmas, and thus of hope for the future. Some process of cleansing must take place if the season of spring is to follow. For this they are waiting.

The Priests indicate the passage of four days since Thomas preached his Christmas sermon. They expect some portent which will mark this day in the Church calendar, as the previous three are marked by St Stephen, the Holy Innocents and St John the Apostle.

NOTES AND GLOSSARY:

Chorus:	see p.10 for a guide to the various alterations that were made to the opening of Part II
the world must be cleansed:	this means both by the birth of Christ, and by the deaths of his martyrs
elder and may:	both bushes, which by their early blossoming symbolise the promise of spring
banner:	these banners offer a pictorial reminder of the three days which have passed since Christmas. They also add a welcome splash of colour and movement after the very static episode of the Sermon
Princes moreover . . . :	see the Bible, Psalm 119:23, and Mark 15:56
he kneeled:	'he' is St Stephen. See the Bible, Acts 7:60. These words of forgiveness are reported to be the last spoken by Stephen as he was stoned to death
Introit:	a versicle or sentence, using words from the Bible, chanted as the priest approaches the altar to celebrate Eucharist. In each case the Introit has been compiled from verses which recall martyrdom
St John:	to whom the second day after Christmas is sacred
In the midst of the congregation . . . :	see the Bible, Psalm 22:22: 'I will declare thy name unto my brethren; In the midst of the congregation will I praise thee'
That which was from the beginning . . . word of life:	this whole phrase is taken from the Bible, 1 John 1:1

Holy Innocents: the infants slain by Herod (see the Bible, Matthew 2:16) in his attempt to kill the infant Christ

Out of the mouths of very babes: from the Book of Common Prayer, Psalm 8:2: 'Out of the mouths of very babes and sucklings hast thou ordained strength . . .'

As the voice of many waters: from the Bible, Revelation 14:2

They sung as it were a new song: see the Bible, Revelation 14:3 and Psalm 98:1

The blood of thy saints: see the Bible, Revelation 6:10

And there was no man to bury them: see the Book of Common Prayer, Psalm 79:3

Avenge, O Lord: from the Bible, Deuteronomy 32:43. See also Milton's sonnet on the massacre of the Piedmontese which begins 'Avenge, O Lord, thy slaughtered saints . . .'

In Rama: see the Bible, Matthew 2:18 and Jeremiah 31:15

Rejoice we all, keeping holy day: Psalm 42:4: 'I went with them to the house of God, with the voice of joy and praise, with a multitude that kept holyday'

he offereth for sins: see the Bible, John 1:29: 'Behold the Lamb of God, which taketh away the sin of the world'

He lays down his life: see the Bible, John 10:11: 'The good shepherd giveth his life for the sheep'

retrospection: looking back

sordid particulars: very appropriate words to herald the arrival of the Knights

---

Part II: Knights, Priests, Archbishop, lines 63–205 (pages 61–72)

Spurning the priests' civil offer of hospitality, the Knights accuse Becket of treason, rebellion, and ingratitude towards the King. They claim Becket spoke against Henry to the Pope and to the King of France, and that, when pardoned for this, he showed his rancour by questioning the legality of Prince Henry's coronation. Becket denies these charges; the Pope has condemned the bishops for their part in the coronation, and only the Pope can undo it.

The Knights claim to bear a command from Henry that Becket must leave England. Thomas refuses, warning that not even the threat of death can shake him.

NOTES AND GLOSSARY:

servant, tool, jack: the language used is deliberately coarse and insulting to the Archbishop; the Knights are trying to make Becket lose his temper

tradesman's son:	again the Knights are trying to anger Becket. They sneer at him for not being a gentleman. While Becket was a merchant's son, he was certainly not lowly born
saving my order:	'leaving on one side my duty as a priest in Holy Orders'. The Knights play upon the word 'saving' a few lines later
your new coat:	Becket makes them confess their total loyalty to King Henry, then implies by 'new' loyalty that this is a betrayal of what should be every man's first allegiance—that which is owed to God
soiled:	dirtied
the old fox:	earlier there were references to hawks, and to a stag at bay. The Knights here use yet another metaphor which reminds us that they are hunting Becket
dissension:	quarrel
endued:	granted
former privilege:	given back all the rights and titles he had before the quarrel
clemency:	mercy
See:	the proper name for the area over which an Archbishop has jurisdiction
suspending:	that is, the Archbishop of York and the Bishops of London and Salisbury, for conducting the coronation of Prince Henry
anathema:	a formal ecclesiastical curse, involving excommunication
evince:	overcome
redounds:	reflects
mendicant:	beggar
attainting:	depriving of rights by conviction for treason, as Becket did with York, London and Salisbury
not against me . . . But the Law of Christ's Church:	Becket sees that the struggle is not a personal matter, but involves the State seeking supremacy over the Church
malfeasance:	bad faith, illegal deeds

Part II: Chorus, Archbishop, Priests, lines 206–77 (pages 72–6)

The Chorus gives vent to feelings of horror, nausea and hysteria. The world seems at this moment to be corrupted, perverse, filled with decay. The women's nervous excitement makes them hypersensitive, as they realise how helpless they are to assist Becket or to play any part in his agony except that of onlookers.

The Archbishop sympathises and tries to console them; time will dull the memory of their agony.

Becket refuses the exhortations of the Priests to escape from the Knights, but they seize him and force him into the cathedral.

NOTES AND GLOSSARY:

subtile: subtle, over-sensitive

fluting: strange-sounding bird song

scaly wings: like those of flying reptiles from the very early days of the world's evolution

jackass: Eliot may mean either the male ass, which makes a raucous laughing noise; or the laughing jackass, an Australian kingfisher whose cry resembles human laughter

jerboa: a desert-dwelling animal that moves with a jumping motion

loon: a diving bird, which utters a human-sounding cry

ingurgitation: a greedy swallowing motion

kite: a bird of the hawk family

mews: a street or yard containing stables

byre: a cowhouse

potentates: men who possess power

the lust of self-demolition: desire for suicide

figure: symbol, pattern

vespers: evening prayers

consummation: fulfilment, conclusion

Part II: Chorus, Priests, Archbishop, Knights, lines 278–422 (pages 76–84)

Whilst the scene changes to within the cathedral, the Chorus expresses a fear of death and of the awful nullity and emptiness of the after-life. It prays for help.

Thomas refuses to allow the Priests to bar the cathedral doors. The battle is no longer to be fought by physical violence or resistance. The partly drunken Knights make one last demand that he should undo all the deeds which have antagonised the King. Becket refuses and they kill him.

The Chorus feels soiled by a mysterious sense of blood everywhere, and prays to be cleansed.

NOTES AND GLOSSARY:

Dies Irae: (*Latin*) literally, 'the day of wrath, or judgement'. The *Dies Irae* is a Latin funeral hymn, supposedly written by Thomas de Celano between AD1200 and 1300. The first verse of this hymn runs as follows

Dies Irae, dies illa
Solvet saecula in favilla
Teste David et Sybilla

Its unusual and strongly accented rhythm is echoed by the Chorus at the beginning and the conclusion of its speech (pp.76 and 78)

Void: absolute emptiness or nothingness. The Chorus fears this may be the state to which it will be condemned after the Last Judgement has been passed

tree: the Cross

impending: drawing near

sanctuary: sacred place. See the note on Part I line 1

stay: security

the triumph of the Cross: a victory not achieved by struggle on a physical level, but by willing sacrifice as in Christ's acceptance of martyrdom by crucifixion

Daniel: in the Bible, Daniel, 6:16-20, tells how the prophet was thrown into a den of lions, but through God's protection escaped unharmed. The rhythm of these verses by the Knights is influenced by a poem called 'Daniel Jazz', written by the American author Vachel Lindsay in 1920. Its jazziness here suggests the tipsy state the Knights are in

the mark of the beast: in the Bible, Revelation 13:16 and 19:20, and Daniel 7:3-11 speak of the end of the world and of the chaos which will precede it, when a mysterious 'beast' will have a fearful period of domination and all will receive its 'mark'

the Lamb: in the book of Revelation the Lamb is the symbolic force of good which opposes the Beast. The Lamb is usually taken to be Christ, and 'the blood of the Lamb' refers to the blood shed by Christ in atonement for man's sins

Absolve: pardon, set free

arrogated: claimed unjustly

appropriated: stolen

Reginald, three times traitor: Reginald Fitz Urse is supposed to have owed a feudal duty to Becket, to have been his 'temporal vassal'

desecrating: committing a crime within the precincts of a holy place, profaning

renegade: one who has broken his faith

a land of barren boughs . . .: in Dante's poem *The Divine Comedy* there
is a description of a forest of trees whose boughs
bleed when they are broken ('Inferno', 13, 31-46)

Part II: The Four Knights, lines 423-580 (pages 84-90)

The Knights step out of the historical events of the play and address the
audience on the subject of Becket's murder. They argue that they
behaved unselfishly, since they have nothing to gain for themselves from
Becket's death. Becket betrayed the King's trust by not using his power
as Archbishop to help Henry to bring peace to the land. Hence they
have helped further the ultimate cause of democracy, since in killing
Becket they helped to assert the rights of the civil power over those of
the Church, a state of affairs now accepted as desirable by the modern
world. And Becket, they suggest, was selfish to the point of insanity. He
wanted martyrdom and deliberately provoked them into killing him.
Hence they conclude that he must have been mad, and his death was an
act of suicide.

NOTES AND GLOSSARY:
disinterested: free from selfish motives
emotional clap-trap: false arguments based on sentiment rather than
reason
Matilda . . . Stephen: see p.6
irruption: invasion
ascetic: morally strict
incompatible: mutually contradictory
condemn an Archbishop by Act of Parliament: as happened with Thomas
Cranmer, Archbishop of Canterbury, in 1556
egotism: interest only in oneself
unimpeachable: which cannot be doubted
he had not long to live: the Messenger reported earlier in the play that
Becket said to Henry, 'My Lord . . . I leave you as
a man whom in this life I shall not see again' (p.16)
inference: deduction, conclusion to be drawn
exasperated: provoked, deliberately made angry

Part II: Priests, Chorus, lines 580-649 (pages 90-4)

The Priests lament the loss of their guide and protector, but realise that
his death will bring a new strength to the Church. They envisage the
murderers driven to the corners of the earth, unable ever to justify what
they have done. They pray that Becket will remember them in his new
state of glory, a state for which they praise God.

The Chorus takes up the theme of praise. Becket's martyrdom has brought fresh glory not only to Canterbury but to all mankind. Forgiveness is begged for the cowardice and blindness of mankind, and acknowledgement made of the role of God's martyrs in working for salvation. Finally the Chorus begs for the blessing of St Thomas.

NOTES AND GLOSSARY:

bereft: deprived by death

Triumphant in adversity: gaining victory out of difficulties

Brittany: a region on the North Atlantic coast of France

the Gates of Hercules: the old name for the Straits of Gibraltar

Saracen: Muslim, more particularly one of those who opposed the Christian crusaders in the medieval wars for the Holy Land

filthy rites: the Saracens in fact had no such rites

libidinous: lustful

Aquitaine: a province of France

Te Deum: a religious hymn of praise, the first words of which, in Latin, are *Te Deum laudamus*: 'We praise thee, O God'

affirm: prove

Iona: an island in the Hebrides, off the west coast of Scotland, famous as the site of a very early and important Christian settlement and monastery

deprivation: enforced loss

Part 3

Commentary

The nature of the play

Murder in the Cathedral seems to be a historical play; it deals with the events leading up to the death of Thomas Becket. Yet there are significant differences between Eliot's play and an ordinary history play, just as there are differences between his treatment of Becket's death and that which we find in the contemporary chronicles. *Murder in the Cathedral* was commissioned for performance in Canterbury Cathedral as part of a religious festival. Certain aspects of the style, the stagecraft and the treatment of character in the play are influenced by its origins.

The murder of Becket obviously made an appropriate subject for a play to be performed at Canterbury Cathedral, the very building in which the deed occurred. Through the centuries the memory of Becket has been revered at Canterbury. St Thomas was, for many centuries, the most famous of all English martyrs; people came from all over Europe to worship at his shrine, where many miracles are reported to have taken place.

Eliot could assume that most of his audience were familiar with Becket's story. He did not have to spend time establishing the identity of his characters or filling in the background. But this very familiarity could work against the playwright. The audience would be aware right from the start that the Archbishop was to be murdered, and that his murderers would escape. The handling of both plot and character called for careful and even unusual treatment. This suggested that he should not write a 'straight' history play, merely re-telling the events leading up to Becket's death. The nature of Eliot's mind and personality made this unlikely too. He was a poet, not a dramatist, at this time. He had recently undergone a spiritual crisis and discovered Christianity after a period of religious doubt. Thus all his attention was focused upon the inner nature of the drama in Becket rather than upon the politics and the history of his death. It is as the centre of a private drama that we appreciate Eliot's protagonist.

Eliot chose a dramatic style and structure which would allow the development of ideas, and which by its very nature would play down the struggle for power between King and Archbishop. Eliot believed the conflict in Becket centred upon a particular idea—the nature of martyrdom. Eliot's Becket is torn by doubts as to whether he will be fulfilling

God's will if he allows events to lead him to his death, or whether he will be imposing his selfish will upon history.

Clearly such a drama is a long way from an ordinary history play which, whilst it may embody abstract ideas, seeks to make those ideas clear through a vigorous and circumstantial account of politics, personal relationships, and the inter-play of character.

There is another form of drama which deals with historical events, besides the history play. This is the pageant. Pageants present local or popular events through tableaux, or separated dramatic scenes. They do not investigate character or the development of human relationships, for they are more concerned with depicting events than people. Because of their relative simplicity pageants are often performed by amateur groups rather than by professional actors.

Eliot was aware that, for the Canterbury Festival, many of his actors would be amateurs. Although the life of Becket became a matter of national, even of international interest, it was at Canterbury that his memory was particularly cherished. These factors may have led Eliot to include elements of the pageant into the dramatic structure of *Murder in the Cathedral*. Passages such as the procession of the priests with their banners near the beginning of Part II, clearly reflect this.

Eliot's play was to be performed in the chapter house at the cathedral, a building not particularly well suited to the staging of drama. Eliot wisely settled for a plot structure which avoided physical action, large cast, numerous exits, or elaborate scenery.

He combined elements of Greek tragedy with features of the English pageant play to produce a work simple in its outward structure but subtle and original in its inner movement. His treatment is ritualistic rather than realistic. The tone of such a work would naturally be sober, discreet and serious. No extraneous material should be expected in a play of this kind. Thus while the needs of the occasion gave some clear guide lines to the dramatist, they also imposed clear limitations. He had to create sufficient variety to keep the audience attentive, while retaining an overriding atmosphere of dignity and restraint. Lacking direct dramatic experience, Eliot fell back upon his instincts as a poet. He devised a Chorus which set the tone of the verse, and represented common humanity. It served to bridge the gap between the lofty and distant persons of the story and the audience. The Chorus has verse of great variety, into which much of the play's imagery is woven.

In describing the kind of play Eliot wrote in *Murder in the Cathedral* it is helpful to recognise the function of the Chorus in shaping the play. Because there are so few developed characters in this drama, an alternative focus is needed, and this the Chorus supplies.

Eliot's state of mind at the time is also relevant to its structure and to the kind of play he created in *Murder in the Cathedral*. His gradual discovery of Christianity in the years from 1928 to 1935 found him eager to give expression to his new faith. The story of Becket's spiritual struggle and victory gave Eliot a chance to discuss matters close to his private interests. He created a structure which investigates the nature of Christian choice and Christian destiny, which questions the nature of martyrdom, which examines the nature of the relationship between the State and individual conscience, and which scrutinises the place of man in the universe and within God's overall plan.

Murder in the Cathedral is a philosophical drama, owing direct debts to the pageant and to Greek tragedy. In its style and scope it moves away from the traditional history play, replacing breadth of treatment with a concentrated intensity of inner activity.

Themes

The most striking themes in *Murder in the Cathedral* are the nature of martyrdom and Christian sacrifice; the responsibility of the individual for his own spiritual well-being; and the nature of faith.

Martyrdom

Eliot prepares us to accept this difficult theme in two ways. He makes the members of the Chorus, in their ignorance, express a feeling close to one which may be shared by the audience: 'It would not be well if he should return' (p.12). Their timidity, desire to avoid trouble, and anxiety for the bodily well-being of their Archbishop are points with which we can sympathise. Yet the play also reminds us of the greatest of all sacrifices within the Christian view of things—Christ's willing acceptance of death upon the Cross. As the play develops Becket becomes more and more like Christ. And the view of Chorus and audience is developed from belief in the value of bodily safety to acceptance of the necessity to sacrifice the body to matters of the spirit. Thus the Chorus moves from fear to joy, from despair to faith, offering a living demonstration of the efficacy of Becket's martyrdom.

For Becket the issue is to be certain that he gives up his life for the right reason. If he wishes to die because it will bring fame after death, or because he has been driven as far as he can endure, then his death will not, in the highest sense, be a martyrdom:

> A martyrdom . . . is never the design of man; for the true martyr is he who has become the instrument of God, who has lost his will in the will of God, and who no longer desires anything for himself, not even the glory of being a martyr. (Interlude, p.53)

In his sermon preached after he has resolved his spiritual crisis, the

Archbishop makes clear his own and Eliot's attitude to martyrdom. This involves an utter abandonment of self-will and self-interest. Though a man may know he will be killed in pursuit of a certain course of action, and though he may be aware that death in this cause may bring him fame, he must accept the death without ever wishing the glory. This is why the Fourth Tempter disturbs Becket. The Tempter insists on reminding him that people will flock to the martyr's shrine seeking miraculous cures, that Thomas's name will be revered throughout the Christian world. It is tempting to seek death if this lasting fame is to be the reward. But such a quest for death would be 'the greatest treason: To do the right deed for the wrong reason' (1.698, p.47). Becket realises that:

> Servant of God has chance of greater sin
> And sorrow, than the man who serves a king.
> For those who serve the greater cause may make the cause serve
>   them . . . (Part I ll.689–92; p.48)

Becket struggles to reach the point at which he can accept the pure martyrdom regardless on the one side of the pain, and on the other of the glory. Though political or spiritual capital may be made of his death, he must seek to make neither for himself. The risks are terrible, for how may a man know when he has purified his mind so much that it no longer has any desire save for the will of God?

The structure of the play helps us to appreciate Becket's struggle, and its resolution. Each episode builds towards the moment of resolution and clarity. The moment of arrival for Becket, at the end of Part I (after the Fourth Tempter has failed), is dramatically in advance of the moment when the Chorus realises the meaning of his sacrifice (at the very end of the play). Thus Part I shows Becket's struggle, the Sermon gives concentrated expression to his discovery, and Part II shows the Chorus learning to accept the mystery of the Archbishop's death.

It has sometimes been said that *Murder in the Cathedral* is 'mechanical' in its structure. If this means that the play has a logical and inevitable grasp of cause and effect, it may be so. But this ignores the extent to which the audience is involved, with the Chorus, in the painful process of discovery which follows the Archbishop's own moment of clarity. Real struggle is involved, and the structure of the play underlines but does not hamper the expression of this.

'Destiny waits in the hands of God', exclaims the Chorus (Part I, l.42; p.13). This is a view which we might expect of the women of Canterbury, desperate to avoid trouble, and convinced that they can do nothing to help or hinder the course of events:

> For us, the poor, there is no action,
> But only to wait and to witness. (Part I, ll.49–50; p. 13)

We shall soon learn that the true martyr *cannot* himself merely 'wait and witness'. Becket's life and actions have too much significance for him to be able to adopt this passive role.

The Archbishop knows that his life is in danger from the outset:

> . . . when the Archbishop
> Parted from the King, he said to the King,
> My Lord, he said, I leave you as a man
> Whom in this life I shall not see again. (Part I, ll.104-7; p.16)

But may he not wilfully seek to bring death upon himself to achieve the personal glory and reward of sainthood? This would be a worse crime than merely giving in to Henry. Hence, not only Becket's life, but also his soul is at risk.

His case is made more difficult by the pressure which both the Chorus and the Priests put upon him. The Priests desire his leadership and protection:

> We can lean on a rock, we can feel a firm foothold
> Against the perpetual wash of tides of balance of forces of barons
>   and landholders. . . .
>   And when the Archbishop returns
> Our doubts are dispelled. (Part I, ll.130-4; pp.17-18)

Hence, if he is to die, Becket must reconcile himself to depriving his natural dependants within the priesthood of his leadership.

The Priests welcome him back as their leader; the members of the Chorus, conversely, wish him to leave again, so that he may continue (from the safety of France) to be their remote but trusted leader. Thus they may continue their lowly but acceptable state of 'living and partly living':

> O Thomas our Lord, leave us and leave us be, in our humble
>   and tarnished frame of existence, leave us; do not ask us
> To stand to the doom on the house, the doom on the Archbishop,
>   and doom on the world. (Part I, ll.190-1; p.20)

Whether he returns to France or insists on staying in Canterbury some of those dependent upon Becket will be in distress. This outward problem serves, however, to symbolise the more subtle inward pressure, where he may make the right choice for the wrong reason. The inner problem is partly expressed in Becket's first speech in the play:

> They know and do not know, what it is to act or suffer
> They know and do not know, that action is suffering
> And suffering is action. Neither does the agent suffer
> Nor the patient act. But both are fixed
> In an eternal action, an eternal patience

> To which all must consent that it may be willed
> And which all must suffer that they may will it,
> That the pattern may subsist . . . (Part I, ll.208–15; p.22)

This speech suggests that every cause affirms an effect, and every effect has a cause. Nothing exists in an independent vacuum. Whilst it implies the dependence of the poor women (the patients) upon Becket (the agent) it suggests that his own view of his role may contain an element of pride. This confirms what the Messenger has already told us:

> His pride always feeding upon his own virtues
> Pride drawing sustenance from impartiality,
> Pride drawing sustenance from generosity
> Loathing power given by temporal devolution,
> Wishing subjection to God alone. (Part I, ll.118–22; p.17)

Thus even his best and most generous impulses are tainted with human weaknesses. The play shows him struggling through the four temptations to overcome these weaknesses, and having done so shows, in Part II, how he triumphantly faces the martyrdom he has now earned. Thus Becket himself is both 'patient' and 'agent'.

Becket only realises through the Fourth Tempter, that pride is the enemy he has to conquer. Now comes the final moment of crisis and self-realisation:

> Is there no way, in my soul's sickness
> Does not lead to damnation in pride? . . .
> Can sinful pride be driven out
> Only by more sinful? Can I neither act nor suffer
> Without perdition? (Part I, ll.584–8; pp. 42–3)

Here he sheds the desire to be 'agent', to will his own death; he no longer believes he can 'turn the wheel on which he turns'. And thus Becket comes to his spiritual awakening, realising that the only way he can reach the still centre of the turning wheel of life is to yield to the mover, to the point that is not himself. Becket, then, yields the last stronghold of selfhood to God's will, and is truly prepared for martyrdom.

The difference between the state of the true martyr and that of the man merely seeking his own glorification is difficult to demarcate. Part II of *Murder in the Cathedral* shows that Becket has achieved this sublime state. He can accept his death without fear, yet without striving to make personal or political capital from it. In this, together with his perfect acceptance of the will of God, he shows what true martyrdom must be, and what the struggle must be in any human being before he is able to achieve this state of mind.

Responsibility

This theme is introduced by the Chorus. The women flock to the Cathedral under the influence of a vague but pressing sense of fear; their first motion is to seek sanctuary in the traditional authority of the Church. For Becket, of course, there can be no such sanctuary. His responsibility is to define and to change the grounds on which the authority of the Church is founded.

The unease of the women is as much at being 'compelled to witness' as at what they will witness. Just as Becket has to learn his responsibility within martyrdom, the Chorus members have to learn theirs within everyday life. They will not be allowed to avoid the anguish of misunderstanding, of being forced to witness the Archbishop's suffering and doubt. Only through the responsibility of witness can they come to the fulfilment which they are granted at the end of the play.

Their imagery is full of the detail of normal everyday life: apples stored, the labourer kicking off muddy boots, ploughing, harvest, seasonal change. They believe that:

> For us, the poor, there is no action,
> But only to wait and witness . . . (Part I, ll.49–50; p.13)

Yet as the action unfolds they are drawn closer to the centre of things, and into a growing understanding of Becket's struggle. They are changed morally for the better by their acceptance of the role of responsible witnesses:

> We did not wish anything to happen.
> We understood the private catastrophe,
> The personal loss, the general misery,
> Living and partly living . . .
> But this, this is out of life, this is out of time,
> An instant eternity of evil and wrong . . .
> (Part II, ll.404–7 and 417–18; p.83)

Here, at the moment of Becket's death, the women of the Chorus accept their responsibility as witnesses; 'We are soiled by a filth that we cannot clean . . .' (l.419; p.84). In the end their translation from 'patients' into 'agents' is complete. They have the last, and perhaps the most moving speech in the play:

> We praise Thee, O God, for Thy glory displayed in all the creatures
>   of the earth,
> In the snow, in the rain, in the wind, in the storm; in all of
>   Thy creatures, both the hunters and the hunted.
> For all things exist only as seen by Thee, only as known by Thee,
>   all things exist

Only in Thy light, and Thy glory is declared even in that which
denies Thee; the darkness declares the glory of light.
(Part II, ll.617-20;p.92)

This subsumes the images of harsh and of corrupted nature by which
the women's speeches are marked earlier (e.g. Part II, ll.206-45;
pp.73-4), and their fear of 'emptiness, separation from God' (Part II,
l.292; p.77) yields to the recognition of their place in the responsible
total scheme of things:

Forgive us, O Lord, we acknowledge ourselves as type of the
common man,
Of the men and women who shut the door and sit by the fire
(Part II, ll.637-8; p.94)
We acknowledge our trespass, our weakness, our fault; we
acknowledge
That the sin of the world is upon our heads; that the blood of the
martyrs and the agony of the saints
Is upon our heads. (Part II, ll.643-5; p.94)

This makes Eliot's women of Canterbury rare among dramatic choruses.
They are full participants and they undergo change in the course of the
play. Usually the Chorus retains the same attitude throughout the play.
It is clearly through the theme of responsibility, and the gradually
enhanced discernment of the burden to be borne, that this surprising
and moving development occurs. The women have witnessed a desperate struggle and a great spiritual victory in Becket and some awareness of its meaning has been forced upon them. Hence their final
utterance has a new note of confidence and joy; it transmutes their own
earlier account of the destructive cycle of the seasons into a harmony of
praise:

Even in us the voices of seasons, the snuffle of winter, the song of
spring, the drone of summer, the voices of beasts and of birds
praise Thee. (Part II, l.627; p.93)

The theme of responsibility is also present elsewhere in the play. The
priests are humanised by their very ordinary sense of responsibility. As
good servants of the Church they take pride in making Becket's room
ready, in having his papers in order. Their urgent desire to protect him
from the attack of the Knights, and their paternalistic fussing over the
Chorus, also illustrate their sense of responsibility. But it is a completely limited sense; it lacks a spiritual dimension, an ability to see the
greater issues which are at stake.

The Knights, ironically, seek to share their responsibility for the
crime of Becket's death with the audience: 'we merit your applause;

and if there is any guilt whatever in the matter, you must share it with us'. (Part II, ll.531–3; p.88). Their eagerness to shed the responsibility for their own act degrades them morally by contrast with Becket.

The Tempters offer Becket various kinds of responsibility, each of which had seemed important to Thomas earlier in his career, but which are an evasion of his ultimate responsibility to God. The First Tempter offers friendship with the King, and a return to the old days when the kingdom was at peace. Though Becket easily shrugs this off, we should not underestimate the temptation it offers. Indeed, in normal circumstances it should be the responsibility of each man to seek that peace: Thomas recognises that 'the impossible is still temptation' (Part I, l.319; p.27). But this, in his present crisis, is the awakening of a 'dead world'. The time for such a solution is past.

The Second Tempter suggests that peace would lie in Becket's resuming his temporal responsibility as Chancellor:

Power obtained grows to glory,
Life lasting, a permanent possession. (Part I, ll.334–5; p.27)
To set down the great, protect the poor,
Beneath the throne of God can man do more? (Part I, ll.347–8; p.28)

This power can only be achieved, however, by submission of part of his spiritual authority in a compromise with King Henry, and it is Becket's lonely and difficult task to spurn this lower authority.

The Third Tempter is yet more subtle. He offers Becket the chance to destroy the King's rule in collusion with the Barons. Becket accepts that the idea had occurred to him:

To make, then break, this thought has come before . . .
But if I break, I must break myself alone. (Part I, ll.471–4; pp.36–7)

His refusal is again a matter of accepting a higher responsibility.

The Fourth Tempter offers the use of martyrdom for his own selfish ends. Here civic responsibility is overwhelmed by the more urgent spiritual one. The sin of abusing his own act of sacrifice would damn Becket. In defeating this temptation he makes a leap forward to total acceptance of God's will:

Now is my way clear, now is the meaning plain;
Temptation shall not come in this kind again.
The last temptation is the greatest treason:
To do the right thing for the wrong reason. (Part I, ll.665–8; p.47)

Hence the play is able to link the themes of personal responsibility and of responsibility to the State, and to show how Becket's is the noblest course.

Faith

Murder in the Cathedral presents differing and ascending planes of moral value. Faith is the yardstick by which these planes can be measured.

On the lowest level the Knights and Tempters lack all real faith. The Tempters suggest to Becket that he can break faith with his own sense of integrity and purpose. Their moral nullity is shared by the Knights. (It is easy to see, therefore, why the roles of Knights and Tempters are so often played by the same actors.) The Knights' role as murderers suggests their faithlessness, and their specious arguments after the murder confirm it. They even lack faith in the deed they are doing. The Second Priest realises this when he states of them:

You still shall tramp and tread one endless round
Of thought, to justify your actions to yourselves,
Weaving a fiction which unravels as you weave,
Pacing forever the hell of make-believe
Which never is belief: (Part II, ll.606–10; pp.91–2)

The growth of faith in the women of the Chorus is a marked feature of the play. They begin in confusion, lacking faith in their own judgement, even in the ability of the Church to protect them. They lack faith in the future, on both a temporal and a spiritual plane:

We
Are afraid in a fear which we cannot know, which we cannot face,
which none understands . . . (Part I, ll.186–8; p.20)

They misunderstand Becket's position ('Archbishop, secure and assured of your fate') and their vision darkens as danger increases in Part I:

Man's life is a cheat and a disappointment;
All things are unreal,
Unreal or disappointing: (Part I, ll.604–6; p.44)

Their judgement of the harrowed Becket as 'obstinate, blind, Intent on self-destruction' (Part I, ll.613–14; p.44) shows how little faith they have in a higher spiritual life.

In Part II a growing awareness of Becket's agony leads to growing faith. The Sermon helps to teach them the nature and purpose of martyrdom. The lesson is learned painfully and slowly. The final act of sacrifice by Becket, and their 'consent' to it, leaves them 'torn', 'subdued', 'violated'. But at last they understand, as their final *Te Deum* makes plain.

The Priests also move from doubt to faith through the Archbishop's example. They begin with questions, doubts, disbelief. When these feelings are dispelled it is for the wrong reason:

When the Archbishop returns
Our doubts are dispelled. (Part I, ll.133–4; p.18)

In fact his return will plunge them further into doubts, from which only his death can release them to a new faith: 'the Church is stronger for this action, Triumphant in adversity'. (Part II, ll.589–90; p. 91). They wished him not to 'fight the intractable tide'. Like the Chorus, however, they are inspired by the Sermon to a new awareness. Their recognition of what has happened to Becket—'Now in the sight of God Conjoined with all the saints and martyrs gone before you' (Part II, ll.613–14; p.92)—constitutes an affirmation of faith in the process of martyrdom. The final moments of the play join them with the Chorus in the act of praise which is the positive response of faith to conviction.

The theme of faith naturally finds its fullest expression in Becket. His first words in the play suggest a faith in mysterious processes beyond the mundane and expected, for even the bewilderment of the Chorus, to Becket's ear, has something true in it: 'They speak better than they know, and beyond your understanding' (Part I, l.206; p.21). His concept of the wheel to which all are fixed implies a belief in the Creator who has appointed the due times and stations of man's life, though even he cannot, at this moment, see the precise purpose of things.

The Archbishop's faith is the greater because it is allied to a near-certain knowledge of his death. Any man who believes in a God who wills his murder *must* have great faith. Everyone else in the play acts blindly and hopes all will be well. Becket knows that, in terms of his personal safety, all will not be well. His problem, therefore, is not to find faith, but to make sure that it is directed to the right and highest end. He must throw over faith in his own judgement, and commit himself to a total and simple faith in God's will. To a proud man who has wielded great power this is no easy task. He must transcend a belief in the life of this world, in the supremacy of secular authority, in political alliance, and in assertion of the personal choice. Out of the rejection of these temptations comes the strongest and best faith. When he realises that Christian martyrdom cannot be the effect of a man's will Becket is truly ready to accept his destiny, for now his faith is complete.

Structure of the play

The most noticeable feature of the structure of *Murder in the Cathedral* is its apparent simplicity. Instead of the three or five acts, subdivided into scenes, which are usual in a modern play, it has two Parts, divided by an Interlude comprising a short sermon. Though Eliot implies that

Part II is divided into two scenes, there is absolutely no break in the action.

In Part I Becket is tested; his spiritual state is one of doubt. The Chorus and the Priests also have no clear sense of direction. Part I comes to a climax in the Temptations, which present to Thomas the various possibilities for action. He considers each and having made what we recognise to be the most difficult but correct choice, the first section of the play comes to a natural conclusion: 'Now is my way clear, now is the meaning plain,' he asserts (Part I, l.665; p.47), as he commits himself completely to a rejection of self.

The Interlude permits Becket to speak uninterruptedly from his new position of spiritual authority. His explanation of the nature of martyrdom may hold up the 'action' of the play, but it provides an insight completely necessary to us before we can understand Part II. He explains why he will no longer struggle, why martyrdom cannot be the effect of man's will, and why he is ready at last to accept the responsibility of becoming one of God's chosen martyrs. He also sounds a warning, making it quite clear that physically Part II may seem to us to be an anti-climax unless we are prepared to concentrate on the spiritual rather than the physical action. For if it is already known that he will die, there can be comparatively little tension in watching his dealings with the Knights. Our minds must be concentrated upon the effects, not the causes, of his death. Hence the Sermon prepares the mood and the tone of what is to follow.

Part II, therefore, treats the murder in a ritualistic rather than a realistic manner. The slaughter takes place on stage, but our attention is principally focused upon the Chorus, not on the Knights. Were the play simply about Becket's death this would be an anti-climax. But the speeches of the Priests and the Chorus, revealing their realisation of the purpose of Becket's death, prevent any feeling of disappointment, and underline the conclusion to which the entire work has been planned to lead us.

Simple as it may appear, the structure is carefully plotted. Within the two Parts the separate episodes move us logically and swiftly from event to event, and from state of mind to state of mind. We are always being drawn to the inevitable conclusion. There are no sub-plots or alternative interests to distract us. Eliot also avoids the temptation to make all his action mount to one big scene. In most history plays this point would come with the death of the hero. In Eliot's play, significantly, the very muted and stylised murder comes nearly 250 lines before the end. Again, structure echoes intention. We need to experience the awakening of a new spirit in the Priests and the Chorus if the purpose of Becket's death is to come home to us. The avoidance of physical excitement and of historical colour in telling the story point to the same end—a deeper insight into Becket's mind, and the timeless meaning of his martyrdom.

Most of the characters in the play are much more thinly drawn than is usual in modern drama. It is what they stand for rather than what they are as psychological individuals that matters. We may almost see all the other actors as embodiments of aspects of the debate taking place in Becket's private conscience. Clearly the Tempters are exactly that.

Eliot gives us a brilliant and uninterrupted study of a mind passing through doubt, and through a crisis of pride, into a state of spiritual purity and a surrender of self-will. Few playwrights could have achieved this with Eliot's clarity or his brevity.

He is greatly indebted to his instinctive and entirely appropriate reliance upon the forms and ideas of Greek tragedy. The plays of ancient Athens were semi-religious in their intention, and relied upon a comparatively small cast, using little scenery. These plays investigated the nature of the relationship between man and the gods, and demonstrated the necessity for man's pious acceptance of his fate. Most of the action was embodied in interchanges between the Chorus and the two or three actors. Long formal speeches of description and exposition set the scene, established the mood, and described the emotional state of the participants. All these features are present in *Murder in the Cathedral*.

The Greek plays take events from myth or history as their subject matter; in this too Eliot is close to them. The action commences at a point near its crisis. *Murder in the Cathedral* opens just before Becket returns to England. His quarrel with King Henry, his previous life as Chancellor, his worldly successes as a young man, have to be assumed by the audience from the brief (but very telling) references which are made in the course of the play. By taking only the crisis of Becket's life Eliot achieves great concentration. All our attention is focused upon the moment of Becket's death.

Murder in the Cathedral, like its Greek models, avoids presenting violent action upon the stage. Admittedly Becket's murder takes place before the eyes of the audience, but it is reduced to a stylised ritual. It is wrong to imagine the Knights hacking away excitedly as the blood flows. The Chorus speak 'while the Knights kill him', and Eliot clearly implies by this stage direction that the words are the chief point of interest, not the deed. The murder is represented by stately, formalised blows of the swords, carefully arranged not to take our attention from the Chorus's speech.

The intellectual and poetic nature of the play also explains the lack of depth in the characterisation. Normally we judge a play by the skill with which the individual characters are brought to life, and sustained. *Murder in the Cathedral* does not work like that. We do see into the minds of the Chorus and of Becket, but the other characters are deliberately thin and one-sided. This may at first sight appear a very unexciting play. But if you listen carefully for the subtle developments in attitude by the Chorus, the growing confidence of the Archbishop, and the outrageous claims of the Knights for the wicked deed they have done, you will find that there is a sense of excitement and fulfilment.

'Structure' covers two aspects of the play; its general lay-out, and its organised deployment of ideas. In considering its debt to the pageant and to Greek drama we go some way to understanding its general organisation and the kind of play it is. Yet the structure of the ideas is equally vital. Helen Gardner has stated that 'If in the first act the strife is with shadows, in the second act there is no strife at all'.* This criticism certainly points to the fact that the two Parts of *Murder in the Cathedral* are of different kinds, and that the play has an unusual pattern of development.

In Part I Becket returns to Canterbury still unresolved in his spiritual battle. Should he allow himself to be murdered? Will this be a deliberate act of self-aggrandisement? His pride suggests that martyrdom, because it will make men remember him, would be very attractive. The 'action' of Part I, therefore, embraces his temptation and the rejection of the Tempters in their increasing order of danger to him. Thus the play reaches a definite moment of climax when he conquers the Fourth Tempter.

The Sermon changes the pattern of speech from verse to prose, the visual spectacle from drama to disquisition, and the mood from doubt to certainty. It is a daring idea to hold up the play while Becket explains his new state of mind, and prepares the audience for the forthcoming murder. The sermon acts as both summary and forecast. It confirms Becket's readiness to accept martyrdom through his victory over the Tempters, and it warns us that we must prepare ourselves to accept his death in the proper frame of mind. The Sermon is thus the hinge upon which the entire play is hung. Up to a point Helen Gardner was right to say there is no strife in Part II. There is no further battle to be fought, no more temptation to overcome for Becket. But, however inevitable his death, Part II is held together by the sense of awe this event engenders and, equally, by the growing faith of the Chorus. Thus, if Part I is Becket's struggle to achieve absolute faith in God's purpose, Part II is the struggle of the Chorus and the audience to follow Becket's path, and through his example to achieve their own discovery.

The structure of *Murder in the Cathedral* is, then, unusual, but it is perfectly justified in terms of Eliot's intentions.

*Helen Gardner, *The Art of T.S. Eliot*, Cresset Press, London, 1949.

The characters

Murder in the Cathedral is not primarily a play of character. Our attention is focused on Becket's mental state. A drama of the mind, such as this play, is merely confused and distracted by deeply characterised parts for the secondary actors. Yet within the limits set by this requirement, Eliot has achieved sufficient human interest in his figures to make it possible for us to discuss characterisation.

The chorus

Eliot said the success of his play was heavily reliant 'upon the assistance of the Chorus . . . [because] . . . the essential action of the play—both the historical facts and the matter invented—was somewhat limited. . . . The introduction of a chorus of excited and sometimes hysterical women, reflecting in their emotion the significance of the action, helped wonderfully'.

The Chorus is much closer to us than anyone else in the play. The women talk of harvest, of domestic matters, of the passing seasons, and offer a bond of common interest with the spectators. But we notice that fear, hesitation and lack of spiritual insight characterise their early speeches. The women of Canterbury are easily moved by kindness:

Seven years since the Archbishop left us
He who was always kind to his people. (Part I, ll.19–20; p.12)

This characterises their relationship with Becket throughout the play. They depend upon him so strongly as a father and as a priest that Thomas might be forgiven for losing patience with them during his harrowing internal struggle. But he remains their consoler and their teacher. The audience shares with the Chorus, therefore, an admiration for the play's hero. This common bond helps us to accept the spiritual message being offered to the Chorus; it acts as a bridge between the play and the audience. The women's characteristic desire to avoid trouble may strike a note of sympathy from the audience too:

. . . we are content if we are left alone.
We try to keep our households in order . . .
Preferring to pass unobserved. (Part I, ll.25–9; p.12)

Most ordinary people react like this to the dangers brought into their lives by politics, power struggles and national wranglings. The Chorus has an unconscious sense of danger threatening:

. . . I fear disturbance of the quiet seasons:
Winter shall come bringing death from the sea, . . .
                                        (Part I, ll.30–1; p.12)

So their first speech identifies the women clearly as mediators between the audience and the play, as ordinary people filled with fear of the threatening unknown, whose menfolk plough, try to make money, and suffer with the changing weather.

Their second speech (pp.18-21) helps to identify their source of anxiety. The impending return of the Archbishop troubles them. Though they are concerned for his safety, they are even more agitated that his return may disturb their lives. Becket may ask of them some act of moral courage, albeit merely as witnesses. They wish to avoid 'the strain on the brain of the small folk'. Most of us would instinctively react thus in similar circumstances.

Plums, apples, beer, cider, remind us of the timeless, everyday life they lead, and for a moment we almost lean over their shoulder as they gossip at street corners:

We have had various scandals, . . .
We have had laughter and gossip,
Several girls have disappeared
Unaccountably, and some not able to.
(Part I, ll.177-81; p.20)

The touch of whimsical humour in the last two lines brings the women of Canterbury very close to us.

Eliot establishes their place as 'patients', as inactive but necessary witnesses in Becket's own inward drama. The members of the Chorus stress their own desire for inactivity; Becket shows us how even this can be part of a pattern:

They know and do not know, what it is to act or suffer
They know and do not know, that action is suffering
And suffering is action. Neither does the agent suffer
Nor the patient act. But both are fixed
In an eternal action, an eternal patience
To which all must consent. . . .
(Part I, ll.208-13; p.22)

We realise that the Chorus is a vital part of the play, not just a group of women who reassure us by their normality and likeness to ourselves. Hence if these women are important as witnesses of Becket's struggle, so are we.

The sense of hysteria in the Chorus grows as the shadowy presence of the Tempters is cast across it:

. . . the air is heavy and thick
Thick and heavy the sky. And the earth presses up against our feet.
(Part I, ll.601-2; p.43)

The womens' judgement is corrupted by their distress, for they say of their beloved Archbishop:

> This man is obstinate, blind, intent
> On self-destruction,
> Passing from deception to deception,
> From grandeur to grandeur to final illusion,
> Lost in the wonder of his own greatness,
> The enemy of society, enemy of himself.
>
> (Part I, ll.613–18; p.44)

Eliot does well to make them express such a sentiment at this moment of crisis. It raises a question the audience is bound to ask about Becket's motivation in seeking death. By putting similar notions into the heads of the Chorus, he again draws the audience into the play through their agency. When the Chorus is convinced of the rightness of Becket's decision, the audience too will be convinced.

The link between the Chorus and Becket is emphasised as the play progresses. Each needs the other in order that the grand purpose of the martyrdom may be fulfilled. Whilst the Archbishop apprehends their value, the women only very slowly realise their own share of the impending act. By the end of Part I they can at least see that the fate of Becket is closely bound with their own, even this being a development from their state at the play's opening:

> O Thomas Archbishop, save us, save us, save yourself that we may be saved;
> Destroy yourself and we are destroyed. (Part I, ll.663–4; p.47)

This plea comes exactly halfway through the play, representing the halfway stage of the Chorus's development to full understanding. It comes when Becket first sees his way clear, when he accepts that he is now ready to take the responsibility of martyrdom. His realisation and the Chorus's dimmer awareness of a change make a moment of strong dramatic tension upon which to end Part I.

Part II opens, like Part I, with a speech from the Chorus, invoking the seasons through images of farming, housekeeping and nature. The Chorus now realises that the world must be cleansed by some act of sacrifice, an idea absent from its speech in Part I; it shows that it has begun a spiritual progress:

> The world must be cleaned in the winter, or we shall have only
> A sour spring, a parched summer, an empty harvest.
>
> (Part II, ll.16–17; p.57)

The women see that 'death in the Lord' renews and cleanses the world. This is further than they were ever able to see in Part I. Becket's Sermon has clearly had its effect. Again we, the audience, feel that we have shared the Chorus's insight.

The women's sense of the need for a cleansing grows as Part II progresses. In their next speech, 'I have smelt them, the death bringers', their hypersensitive feelings plunge us into a world of riot and corruption. Yet they reveal a new sense of their own share in the world's destiny:

> What is woven on the loom of fate
> What is woven in the councils of princes
> Is woven also in our brains, our veins,
> Is woven like a pattern of living worms
> In the guts of the women of Canterbury. (Part II, ll.229–33; p.73)

They no longer beg Becket to flee or abandon them to their torpid little ordinariness as they did in Part I. They have 'consented', accepted the necessity of bearing witness with Becket. They now wish to share with him the act of prayer:

> . . . pray for us that we may pray for you, out of our shame.
> (Part II, l.246; p.74)

Now they have moved to a higher level of awareness than that of the Priests. This sense of *development* in the moral awareness of the Chorus is one of the most remarkable features of *Murder in the Cathedral*.

The horror of the murder draws them back to their imagery of cleansing. They sense an irreversible change brought about by Becket's death, by a movement forward in their own spiritual awareness:

> How can I ever return, to the soft quiet seasons? . . .
> But this, this is out of life, this is out of time,
> An instant eternity of evil and wrong.
> We are soiled by a filth that we cannot clean . . .
> (Part II, ll.401, 417–19; pp.83–4)

At last full recognition comes to them; their imaginations are washed, cleansed by Becket's sacrifice. The most remarkable testimony to the value and meaning of his action lies in their recognition of their purpose and condition. These women, who at the outset of the play were so lost, so limited, so spiritless, can now truly see:

> We acknowledge our trespass, our weakness, our fault; we
>   acknowledge
> That the sin of the world is upon our heads; that the blood of the
>   Martyrs and the agony of the saints
> Is upon our heads. (Part II, ll.643–5; p.94)

Thus their purpose in the play as 'patients', as witnesses who cannot act but who must suffer and learn through suffering, is achieved. Their role as spokesmen for the audience unites us with them in their final act of confession and worship.

The Priests

The Second Priest is the most human, the First is the most factually minded, and the Third Priest is closest to awareness of spiritual concerns. Essentially, however they operate as necessary voices of contrast between the humble tones of the Chorus and the lofty statements of Becket. Their individualising traits are strongest in Part I, where Eliot is still drawing us into the dramatic debate. Here the Second Priest shows pride and concern in having Becket's room ready for him, and reproves the Chorus as 'foolish immodest babbling women'. The worldly-wise First Priest recognises Becket's pride, but quite mistakes its direction and value. Even in Part II he cannot quite apprehend the nature and effect of the Archbishop's sacrifice:

> The Church lies bereft
> Alone, desecrated, desolated, and the heathen shall build on the
> ruins . . . (Part II, ll.586-7; pp.90-1)

The Third Priest, more in tune with the mystical nature of the sacrifice, believes that 'the Church is stronger for this action', however.

Thus they retain the interest of the audience through their individual responses without obtruding upon the true centre of attention. Their concern for Becket's bodily safety at the time of the murder also helps to create tension and to draw the audience into closer involvement with it.

The Tempters

The First Tempter is the voice of nostalgia for a dead past. He has a seductive turn of imagery, and a free and easy way of talking: 'Old Tom, gay Tom, Becket of London'. He suggests a character not too troubled by morality, and in love with the things of this world, which he is able to make sound dangerously attractive. He lards his speech with proverbs and familiar sayings: 'A nod is as good as a wink'; 'The safest beast is not the one that roars most loud'; 'your goose may be cooked'. As Becket says, he represents 'leave-well-alone, the springtime fancy'. For those of the audience who know the old medieval morality plays his speech patterns and his use of rhyme have a familiar ring, while his imagery of gracious living is a poignant memory of Becket's days as Chancellor, before the quarrel with King Henry.

The Second Tempter is more urbane. He deferentially suggests that

Becket may have forgotten him; he flatters the Archbishop as a 'master of policy', and he is able to twist words into bearing his own meaning by sliding over illogicalities and difficulties:

> . . . thrive on earth and *perhaps* in heaven . . .
> Real power
> Is purchased at price of a *certain* submission.

'Perhaps' and 'certain' seem to detract from the urgency of the higher things for which Becket is striving; these words belittle the life to come in favour of what a man can achieve in this world. Hence he is astute but without moral insight. Whereas the First Tempter is a gay court butterfly, the Second is a wily politician.

The Third Tempter claims to be a 'rough, straightforward Englishman', but like many people claiming to lack subtlety, he is in fact deeply devious. He appeals to Becket's sense of national pride, wishing to use the Archbishop for his own political ends. His argument that 'Endurance of friendship does not depend Upon ourselves, but upon circumstance' is cynical. Since Thomas cannot recapture the King's favour, he should in self-defence help to destroy Henry's authority. He uses words like 'liberty', 'advantage', 'intelligent interest' very much as many modern politicians use them as spurious attractions to draw an audience into sympathy with a heartless cause. These devices hide a policy of schism, hatred and division.

The Fourth Tempter is the most subtle and dangerous. There is a smoothness about him which exceeds the others. Perversely, he chooses the approach of being honest; indeed, he implies that the other Tempters were cheats whom Thomas did well to reject. The Fourth Tempter is almost an echo of the Archbishop's own mind; he possesses considerable wisdom and experience, not seeking to cover up the unpleasant side of things, and ready even to admit that martyrdom may hold dangers and disappointments. He embodies the distinction between true and false martyrdom. It is Becket's recognition of his essential falseness that enables Thomas finally to see his way clear. The Tempter offers him fame after death; only by rejecting that last selfish motive can Thomas accept his true destiny, whatever it may be. The Tempter's power lies in his apparent honesty, his closeness to the Archbishop's own thoughts. Thus he actually echoes Becket's own words (compare Part I, ll.208–17 with ll.591–9).

The Knights

In many productions of *Murder in the Cathedral* the parts of the Knights and of the Tempters are played by the same actors. This gives irony to the meanings of the characters. There are comparisons and points of contact between them. The First Knight, like the First Tempter, emerges as a bluff, limited man, capable of chairing a meeting, but not wishing to speak at it: 'I am a man of action and not of words!' He has a down-to-earth sense of humour—'business before dinner'—which echoes the Tempter's 'The easy man lives to eat the best dinners'.

The Second and Third Knights are, like the equivalent Tempters, politicians. The Third Knight seeks for easy sympathy with the audience; '. . . if we seemed a bit rowdy, you will understand why it was; and for my part I am awfully sorry about it. . . .' (p.85). He suggests that 'reasonable people' will have to agree with the slaughter of Becket, and as we listen to his affable-sounding prose we almost agree.

As the Fourth Tempter was the most subtle in his arguments, so is the Fourth Knight. His claim that Becket was 'a monster of egotism' who was put away for the good of the State is the more dangerous because it is a half-truth rather than an outright lie. Becket was indeed dangerous to the authority which King Henry wished to exert. The Fourth Knight is able to take a ridiculous question like 'Who killed the Archbishop?' and, in only thirty lines, make a convincing claim that Becket to all intents and purposes killed himself. Even the 'evidence' he cites is true. It is the perverse use to which he puts his facts which makes him particularly insidious.

Although the Knights appear only in Part II, and the outcome of their mission is already known, they are capable of surprising us and holding our attention. As with the Priests they are not deeply characterised, but they convey sufficient sense of individuality for the purposes they serve in the play.

Thomas Becket

The actor Robert Speaight, who first played the part of Becket, had this to say about his reactions on first reading it over:

> My initial feeling was one of vague disappointment. There could be no doubt of the play's originality, nor of the beauty of the choral writing. But where was Becket? He appeared to me a very passive protagonist. Assailed by the tempters, importuned by the Chorus, harassed by the Priests and murdered by the Knights, he had little to do—or so it seemed—but to go forward to a predetermined fate. . . .*

The actor changed his mind as he grew to understand the part, and to appreciate Becket's internal struggle. Yet his initial reaction is characteristic of a criticism often levelled at the part of Becket in *Murder in*

*From *T.S. Eliot. A symposium for his seventieth birthday*, ed. N. Braybrooke, Hart-Davis, London, 1958, p.71.

the Cathedral. It is said that Eliot cannot show much character in the
Archbishop because he portrays him at a moment so near the crisis in
his affairs that we understand nothing of his past life, and cannot expect
to see any development in him. Is he a one-dimensional figure, the mere
embodiment of the abstract idea of martyrdom?

If, like Robert Speaight, we study the role more closely, we realise that
there is development. Becket's first entry raises the intellectual quality
of the poetry. Previously the Chorus has expressed vague fears in essentially humble images, and the Priests have appeared fussy and too concerned with everyday matters. Becket is quickly established as a
sensitive, far-sighted man, concerned with matters spiritual and eternal.
Yet his courtesy in dealing with Priests and Chorus is most marked; he
is no visionary with his head in the clouds. We mark his cheerfulness in
adversity, yet when occasion demands he can show a brusque temper
which indicates that he once held the rule of the kingdom in his power:

> . . . shall I, who keep the keys
> Of heaven and hell, supreme alone in England,
> Who bind and loose, with power from the Pope,
> Descend to desire a punier power?
> Delegate to deal the doom of damnation,
> To condemn kings, not serve among their servants,
> Is my office. No! Go. (Part I, ll.376–82; p.31)

He is brought to life by the firmness of his moral stance, coupled with
his gentle insight into the weakness and needs of the Chorus, and with
the misunderstandings of his Priests. Inwardly he suffers much. When
the Third Tempter affirms that Becket can now never be reconciled with
King Henry, he draws from Becket an anguished cry; 'O Henry, O my
King', and we remember that history has it that Henry was the only
man Becket ever really loved. His admission of the desire to bring down
vengeance on those who have thwarted him also helps to humanise him.

He speaks with a wisdom and experience, which has not lost its
memory of the glorious past:

> Thirty years ago, I searched all the ways
> That lead to pleasure, advancement and praise.
> Delight in sense, in learning and in thought,
> Music and philosophy, curiosity,
> The purple bullfinch in the lilac tree,
> The tilt-yard skill, the strategy of chess,
> Love in the garden, singing to the instrument
>
> (Part I, ll.671–7; p.47)

Thus, though there is no time to show us scenes of his earlier life, we are
made aware of Becket as a man who has loved these things. It has been

a struggle to give them up as his conscience has made stronger and stronger demands.

Becket's character does develop, albeit in one sudden leap, after the fourth temptation. In the Sermon, and in the imagery he uses in Part II, there is a new repose and insight. He faces the badgering of the Knights with dignity, as though awareness of the approach of a justified death has stripped him of the need to embroider his speech. His courage is absolute because now his faith is absolute.

He knows his uncompromising answers will enrage the knights, but shows supreme courage in his speeches to them, refusing to have the cathedral doors barred for his own protection:

> . . . We have fought the beast
> And have conquered. We have only to conquer
> Now, by suffering. This is the easier victory (Part II, ll.347–9; p.80)

This certitude of spirit may not in itself be obviously dramatic. It does not lead to the development or surprise which are normal in drama. But it is recognisable as the logical conclusion of the struggle Becket has undergone, and therefore it creates its own mood of dramatic satisfaction. There can be no doubt that careful and sympathetic study reveals Becket to be subtly characterised and unmistakably the centre of the play.

The verse

T.S. Eliot was among the leaders of an attempt to breathe new life into the English verse play. He explained, in a lecture on his own plays given at Harvard University in 1950, that dramatic verse 'must justify itself dramatically, and not merely be fine poetry shaped into a dramatic form'. The verse should absorb the audience, never distract them. Eliot also believed that certain subjects would be more appropriate to treatment in prose, and that the use of verse in such cases could only be a distraction. He disapproved of mixing verse and prose in the same play, except when the audience was to be deliberately jolted 'violently from one plane of reality to another'. This, of course, is his purpose in the prose passages in *Murder in the Cathedral*. When Becket delivers his sermon, we are held in suspense at a still moment in the drama. The shift from verse to prose helps us accept the purpose of the Sermon as it reveals Becket's thoughts about martyrdom. And when the Knights defend the murder of Becket, in very modern sounding prose, we are jolted into the twentieth century, and made to realise that the 'message' of the play is as real now as it was in the distant past.

Eliot tried to create a flexible and adaptable verse which would not leave the audience feeling it was being hustled from high to low moments. He felt that careful control of rhythm could help to make a verse style which would be acceptable throughout the play. He believed that Shakespeare had this gift, 'a kind of musical design . . . which reinforces and is at one with the dramatic movement.' Such a design checks and accelerates the pulse of our emotions without our knowing it. When verse works like this it 'intensifies' the play. Yet he was eager to avoid imitation of Shakespeare:

> Therefore what I kept in mind was the versification of *Everyman*. . . . An avoidance of too much iambic, some use of alliteration, and occasional unexpected rhyme, helped to distinguish the versification from that of the nineteenth century.

These statements are from Eliot's *Poetry and Drama*. Try to read this in full, as well as the relevant sections of the books by Nevill Coghill and by W.H. Mason which you will find listed in Part 5, Suggestions for further reading.

Eliot says he wanted to get away from the iambic rhythm of Shakespeare's verse. An iambus, or iamb, is a unit of verse in which the rhythm goes from a weak to a strong syllable. Shakespeare's verse commonly couples five of these units into the line, which thus becomes an iambic pentameter (from the Greek word *pente*, five). If we represent a weak beat by the symbol ∪ and a strong one by the symbol —, then an iambic pentameter is represented thus; ∪ — / ∪ — / ∪ — / ∪ — / ∪ — /. The symbol / marks the division of each foot, or separate unit. Thus a typical Shakespearean rhythm is

$$\overset{\cup}{\text{For}} \overset{-}{\text{God's}} / \overset{\cup}{\text{sake}} \overset{-}{\text{let}} / \overset{\cup}{\text{us}} \overset{-}{\text{sit}} / \overset{\cup}{\text{upon}} \overset{-}{\text{the}} / \overset{\cup}{\text{ground}} \overset{-}{} /$$

For God's / sake let / us sit / upon / the ground /

And tell / sad stor/ies of / the death / of kings / (*Richard II*)

Eliot wished to break free from this pattern. The play *Everyman* which he chose as his model was written before the time of Shakespeare, about the year 1500; it is very free in its use of rhythm, mixing long and short lines. *Everyman* uses stress with much less regularity than Shakespeare, and it uses rhyme freely but irregularly. *Everyman* also introduces another technical device which Eliot copies in his play, the device of alliteration, a repetition of the sounds with which certain key words in the line commence. A few lines from *Everyman* will illustrate the freedom of the verse and the alliteration (Everyman is praying for mercy to the Virgin Mary):

> O Mary, pray to the Maker of all thing,
> Me for to help at my ending;
> And save me from the power of my enemy,
> For Death assaileth me strongly.

And, Lady, that I may by means of thy prayer
Of your son's glory to be a partner,
By the means of his passion I it crave;
I beseech you help my soul to save. (lines 597–604)

Eliot added more variety, and his control of the rhythms of his verse
is much more conscious than that of the old play; thus, the opening
Chorus starts in fairly long regularly stressed measures:

Here let us stand, close by the cathedral. Here let us wait.

Are we drawn by danger? Is it the knowledge of safety, that draws
our feet

Towards the cathedral? What danger can be

For us the poor, the poor women of Canterbury? what tribulation

With which we are not already familiar? . . .

These lines are not identical to each other, as they would be in iambic
verse. The number of stresses in each line may change, the amount of
alliteration, and the presence or absence of rhyme. The women of
Canterbury sound rather as though they are making responses in
church—a sound entirely appropriate to their mood at this moment.
Indeed, the rhythms of the church service are never far from the verse
in *Murder in the Cathedral*; the *Dies Irae* and the *Te Deum* are echoed,
and the drunken Knights lurch on to a rhythm in parody of a hymn.
Sometimes the verse stretches out into a chant:

> I have seen
> Grey necks twisting, rat tails twining, in the thick light of dawn.
> I have eaten
> Smooth creatures still living, with the strong salt taste of living
> things under sea; I have tasted
> The living lobster, the crab, the oyster, the whelk and the prawn;
> and they live and spawn in my bowels, and my bowels dissolve
> in the light of dawn.

Here the bewilderment of the women in the shock of expectancy at
Becket's death draws out their lines of verse into a wailing cry of horror.
Contrast this with the deliberately clipped, ironic tones of the Fourth
Tempter, who adds rhyme to his speech to emphasise its pointedness:

> King is forgotten, when another shall come:
> Saint and Martyr rule from the tomb.
> Think, Thomas, think of enemies dismayed,
> Creeping in penance, frightened of a shade.

The play is full of this rhythmic variety. Because the listener's ear never quite knows what to expect next by way of stress, rhyme and alliteration the play conveys a sense of expectancy and tension.

Some other special effects call for mention. Rhythmic contrasts help to characterise the speakers. Thus the women (Part I, 1.184) speak of their 'great fear' and the rhythm runs wild to help express this. The Second Priest answers them:

> What a way to talk at such a juncture!
> You are foolish, immodest and babbling women.
> Do you not know that the good Archbishop
> Is likely to arrive at any moment?

His speech rhythms have a much more regular beat than those of the terrified Chorus, emphasising the difference in their states of mind.

When the Knights enter 'slightly tipsy' to murder Becket, the rhythm takes on a drunken, jazzy quality. Eliot imitates the American writer Vachel Lindsay's (1879–1931) poem 'Daniel Jazz'. The repetitions, the insistent beat, and the rhyme on 'priest' and 'beast' in each clearly marked stanza help the ear to distinguish this as a special dramatic moment, the more so as 'priest' and 'beast' are such unlikely words to find so close together.

Eliot has one more rhythmical surprise for us. We might expect him to copy the rhythms of hymns and of the church liturgy, but surely not those used in a famous detective story! Yet this is what he does in Part I, pages 29–30:

> SECOND TEMPTER
> Power is present, for him who will wield
> THOMAS
> Who shall have it?
> TEMPTER
>   He who will come.
> THOMAS
> What shall be the month?
> TEMPTER
>   The last from the first.
> THOMAS
> What shall we give for it?
> TEMPTER
>   Pretence of priestly power
> THOMAS
> Why should we give it?
> TEMPTER
>   For the power and the glory.

This is copied from the incantation in 'The Musgrave Ritual', by Sir Arthur Conan Doyle (1859–1930)*. In this story each member of a noble family has to repeat an apparently meaningless chant when he comes of age. In fact the chant contains the secret of where the lost crown of King Charles I is hidden. Its rhythms are most strongly marked:

Whose was it?
His who is gone.
Who shall have it?
He who shall come.
What was the month?
The sixth from the first.
Where was the sun?
Over the oak.
Where was the shadow?
Under the elm . . .

Eliot's great admiration for Conan Doyle leads him to echo this question-and-answer ritual concerning a crown when Becket is questioning the Tempter about the nature of worldly power.

The final surprise is of course the shift from verse rhythms into prose. We have seen that Eliot wanted to 'jolt' the audience by this technique. So, at a moment of high tension just after the murder, we are suddenly pushed into the prose rhythms of a board meeting or a parliamentary debate. The shock redoubles the attention with which we listen to the Knights. They dislocate our sense of history with their modern prose, so that we are reminded that Becket's death has a meaning for the twentieth century.

The prose of the Sermon is more controlled, less informal than that which the Knights use. Prose is the natural and proper medium for a sermon. Becket's sermon uses long sentences piled upon each other and carefully balanced. It makes frequent use of question and answer, its language is biblical, slightly 'old-fashioned'. Its carefully constructed prose breaks up the action of the play, gives a time of repose when we may consider the meaning of the events we have seen so far, and be given guidance on what is to come. It serves the dramatist's purpose, and is properly distinguished from the rest of the play by its special rhythms and conventional language.

Imagery

There was little scope for realistic scenery in the chapter house at Canterbury where Eliot's play was first produced. He depended upon

*The Memoirs of Sherlock Holmes, Newnes, London, 1894, p.110.

imagery to provide much of its colour and pictorial quality. Eliot once said that dramatic verse 'must be simply relevant to the action which is going forward; but it should also have depths which can only be penetrated by the reader who studies it again and again.'* This is true of the imagery in *Murder in the Cathedral*. In the opening Chorus, for instance, the women of Canterbury use images of the passing seasons, of ordinary domestic life, of light and darkness, and of growth and decay. The natural images help to draw us, by their familiarity, into the web of the play. The images of passing time and the cycle of nature suggest the continuity of time which links us by a common bond with the women-folk at Canterbury in 1170. Images of tilling the land and tending the house help to show that the speakers are ordinary people, concerned with their own little lives. They provide an imagery of light striving and failing to break in on a pattern of ominous darkness.

Hence, they create an appropriate and informative mood for the play's opening. But they also look forward to the later crisis. Their images gradually build into a pattern which adds to the general meaning of the play. The women must be made to see that their little concerns represent only a tiny corner of God's purpose. They slowly become aware that forces of darkness and of light are at war in their world, and that the cycle of birth and death assumes a new meaning through the sacrifice Becket makes for them. They grow more and more stifled by the corruption which they feel in the presence of the Tempters and the Knights. With Becket's martyrdom, their imagery is purged, and their *Te Deum* recalls each of their previous image patterns to show it in a new state of awareness and beauty. Thus, as their character and intellectual stature develop, so does their imagery.

Becket's imagery is more remote and abstract. The image of the wheel of time to which all men are fixed, and which is moved by God at its still centre, is characteristic of him. Likewise the notion of strife with shadows befits a man who has to wrestle with temptations which spring from within his own conscience and ambition. Becket's imagery fuses the concrete with the abstract. After the departure of the Fourth Tempter when Becket is visibly shaken, he instinctively grasps the abstract and gradually assimilates it into imagery of the world about him:

> The last temptation is the greatest treason
> To do the right deed for the wrong reason . . .
> Thirty years ago I searched all the ways
> That lead to pleasure, advancement and praise . . .

Thus far he has merely stated a general idea, but he has the gift of turn-

---

*'The Need for Poetic Drama', *The Listener*, xvi, No. 411, 25 November 1936, p.994.

ing this into attractive pictures, which show, with great clarity, the desirability of life at court:

> Music and philosophy, curiosity,
> The purple bullfinch in the lilac tree . . .

As befits a statesman, lawyer and cleric, Becket's images are drawn from a wide area. Hawking, philosophy, jousting, and theology all colour the way he thinks and speaks:

> For a little time the hungry hawk
> Will only soar and hover, circling lower . . .
> In the tilt-yard I made many yield . . .
> Never again shall the sea run between the shepherd and his fold . . .

One of the most moving aspects of his character is his sympathy with the Chorus. This expresses itself in the imagery as well as in the attitudes he adopts. When he wishes to console them he employs their own domestic language:

> You shall forget these things toiling in the household
> You shall remember them drowsing by the fire
> When age and forgetfulness sweeten memory
> Only a dream that has been told.

The language and world of the Bible are never far from this devout man's mind:

> They shall find the shepherd here, the flock shall be spared . . .

The imagery of the Tempters matches their function. The First Tempter evokes the physical comforts of Becket's days as Chancellor and court favourite: 'viols in the hall, singing at nightfall, whispering in chambers'. He talks of goose for dinner, lovemaking in the orchard, and music in summer meadows—an undeniably pleasant life. But his imagery under-cuts itself, as in:

> Fires devouring the winter season,
> Eating up the darkness, with wit and wine and wisdom!

The suggestion of over-indulgence, of hellfire 'eating up' the indulgent man, of wine blotting out wisdom, lurk behind the seductive surface of the images, offering a clear warning that this is a temptation to a false paradise.

The Second Tempter, as befits a politician, is more abstract. He talks of ruling 'richly', combining job satisfaction with personal profit, and of 'dressing' state dignity with decorum, as though dignity were some shameful thing which needed clothing before it might be respectable.

While the Third Tempter claims to be a 'rough straightforward

Englishman' and while he certainly does not use rich or graphic images, there is a devious subtlety in his rhetoric which takes their place. There is indeed, something chilling about his insistence upon avoiding colourful or everyday correlatives. He is full of abstracts—'sovereignty', 'advantage', 'liberty', 'tyrannous jurisdiction'; these empty words make him unattractive but no less dangerous.

The Fourth Temper uses subtle and complex imagery. His main theme is that beyond worldly pleasure and political power lies another force which has binding power. Thus the concept of binding, of locking something up, of holding fast, runs through many of his speeches:

> You would wait for trap to snap
> Having served your turn, broken and crushed . . .

> You hold the keys of heaven and hell . . .

> You hold the skein, wind, Thomas, wind
> The thread of eternal life and death . . .

His imagery can make the supremacy of spiritual power sound dangerously attractive:

> Think, Thomas, think of enemies dismayed,
> Creeping in penance, frightened of a shade . . .

The imagery in *Murder in the Cathedral* is as varied as the verse which sustains it. It ranges from delightful images of courtly splendour, through graphic pictures of everyday life, to high religious abstractions. The imagery has been carefully suited to the individual speakers and provides a key to the audience's apprecation of the message behind the dramatic spectacle.

Conclusion

Murder in the Cathedral is a play about martyrdom. Becket's spiritual struggle to accept the fate of a martyr without risking damnation for pride and self-will is accompanied by the bewilderment of the women in the Chorus, which gradually gives way to assurance and comfort as they recognise their salvation in the Archbishop's sacrifice.

The structure of the play echoes the inner nature of the struggle; in Part I Becket must identify and encounter the particular temptations to which his nature is prone: in Part II the murder produces an affirmation of new faith in both Priests and Chorus.

The characterisation of the play is sufficient for Eliot's rather abstract purpose. It engages our interest but does not distract us from the intellectual concerns of the work.

Humble life, changing seasons, light, darkness and fire are the main image patterns in the language of the Chorus. These are well integrated with character and function. The Archbishop's imagery reflects the wide range of his courtly, clerical and legal interests, and he has the ability to make sympathetic assimilation of the Chorus's imagery when he is talking to the women of Canterbury. As the play's theme is worked out, the imagery grows more triumphant, less concerned with decay and corruption.

The verse is based not upon Shakespearean iambic pentameters, but upon the freer verse structure of the old play *Everyman*. Line length, number of stresses in the line, and incidence of rhyme may appear random, but all are marshalled to serve the dramatic and intellectual needs of the play.

Part 4

Hints for study

General

Try to enjoy your reading. Remember that enjoyment is increased by understanding; this will motivate close study of the text.

Remember also that these notes are not a substitute for thorough knowledge of the text. Unless you are properly familiar with the work you are studying you can never respond to it.

Preparing an answer

Follow this drill: *Read*; *Stop*; *Think*; *Plan*.

Read the question carefully. Make sure you know exactly what is being asked. Is the question about character, about plot, poetry, themes? If it has more than one part, what is the relationship between them?

Stop to let the question sink in and to collect your thoughts.

Think about the best use of your notes and quotations as they can be organised to suit the particular question. Don't learn 'model answers' which you are determined to use regardless of the question asked.

Plan your answer on a sheet of rough paper. Jot down words, phrases, ideas which seem relevant. Then arrange these random thoughts into a pattern.

Your essay should have an Introduction, stating your intentions, and giving your argument in brief. Then comes the main body of the essay. Separate paragraphs should deal with each point you raise. The essay should be rounded off with a conclusion.

Your effort will be wasted if the examiner cannot read your writing. Neatness matters, so, however rushed you may be, make sure your work is readable.

Plan to give roughly equal time to each of the questions you have to answer. If you run short of time, present an outline of the missing material, but it is much better not to leave yourself in this situation; aim for the proper number of competent answers rather than one long one and three sketchy pieces.

Leave a few minutes at the end for re-reading your answers. Hurry in an examination creates silly errors. You can cut out many of these if you read through what you have written. Accuracy of expression and grammar are qualities the examiner values.

Study notes

Categories of question you will be asked can be considered under the following headings: character, structure, themes and images, versification, type of play, background.

Unless you have special knowledge of English medieval history you should probably avoid the last of these, though both the historical and theatrical background to *Murder in the Cathedral* should have been part of your general study of the play.

While you may take hints from books you read, you should try to think up ideas of your own. The examiner will not wish to see the same work from everyone in the class. It is *your* mind he is trying to assess.

Keep a notebook which summarises your ideas under the various headings listed above. For instance on 'kind of play' you might jot down notes as follows:

Murder in the Cathedral is liturgical pageant drama, with debts to Greek drama.

(i) Liturgical element: written for Canterbury Cathedral festival, static structure dictated by theme and location of staging; ritualistic elements in versification, use of special rhythms.

(ii) Pageant play: historical background, formality of presentation, restrictions on development of character, selection of incidents.

(iii) Debt to Greek drama: unity of time and place, avoidance of sub-plots, role of Chorus.

(iv) Other features: Eliot's particular use of historical sources, two-part structure split by Sermon, (i) temptation, (ii) resolution.

(v) Conclusion: the play's structure is perfectly suited to the place, occasion and kind, and to Eliot's comparative lack of experience as dramatist.

On the subject of 'themes and images' your notebook might include the following:

(i) Themes: Martyrdom and individual Christian responsibility; the discovery of God's will and the yielding of self to it; the temptations reflect aspects of Becket's life he must now reject; problem of 'the right deed for the wrong reason'.

(ii) Images: (a) *Chorus:* accessible images, drawn from everyday life, changing seasons, light, dark, fire; in excitement or depression, images of corruption or disturbed nature; change from doubt to assurance in peace and victory. (b) *Becket:* lends intellectual weight to imagery; images of time, mutability—the wheel—Becket's ability to assimilate the Chorus's images when he speaks to the women. (You should then make a similar collection and analysis of the images used by (c) the Tempters; (d) the Priests; (e) the Knights.)

Specimen questions and answers

Discuss the role and function of the Chorus in Murder in the Cathedral

Plan

Introduction: Chorus vital to tone; human touch to abstract theme; audience identifies through Chorus; Chorus taken from Greek drama; Eliot's Chorus shows change and development as the women learn to accept Becket's destiny; poetry and imagery of Chorus.

Main body: Greek structure suits pageant play; Chorus's changing viewpoint gives movement to work; Becket's sympathy with Chorus gives humanity; audience's sympathy gives pathos; Chorus learns, helps audience to learn, and thus gives shape to the work. Discuss imagery, type, tone, function; also rhythm and metre.

Conclusion: Chorus vital to play; astute dramatic device to draw audience in, and to direct their responses.

Essay

The Chorus is vital to the structure and meaning of *Murder in the Cathedral*. The play's moral theme is reflected in the women's awakening, its imagery receives fullest expression through them, and its structure rests upon the difference in their awareness in the two Parts.

The Chorus derives from Greek drama, where the number of actors was limited, and where the interchanges of dialogue and ideas took place between the Chorus and the principal actors. Its function was thus to act as commentator and sounding-board. Through the fears, hopes and expectations of the Chorus the audience was led to understand the feelings of the hero, and the attitude of the playwright to his subject.

T.S. Eliot, having to write for the comparatively limited resources of the Canterbury Festival, was naturally drawn to such an economical structure. Yet he manages to create a Chorus which fulfils all the requirements of his Greek models, and which has the added interest of making a positive shift in its attitude—something not often present in the earlier Chorus. Eliot's Chorus provides the principal medium of expression for imagery in the play. The themes of ordinary continuing domestic rural life, of moral doubt, and final Christian acceptance of death and martyrdom, come out clearly in its verse.

The rhythms of the Chorus's speech vary with the type and intensity of its emotions, though *Everyman* is the common basis of all the play's versification. The Chorus has great variety and fluidity of rhythm, which in turn lends freshness of interest to the rather intellectual drama of ideas.

Because they change and develop, the women of Canterbury give a clear outline to the moral purpose and direction of the play. They are given the last word; their *Te Deum* at the end of Part II demonstrates that the message of Becket's sacrifice in martyrdom has been understood.

Though *Murder in the Cathedral* has had success in the professional theatre it was originally written for a cast which included amateur actors, of whom Eliot could not make great demands. The play was to be performed in a hall which did not lend itself to much physical action, numerous exits and entrances, or a large cast. These factors influenced Eliot's choice of a Greek-style Chorus as presenter and 'patient'. The relationship between the Chorus and Becket does not demand physical action; the playwright can use his gifts as poet to forward his plot and enrich the texture of his play by skilful use of imagery.

The subject of Becket's martyrdom lent itself to a treatment resembling that of a pageant. It could be reduced to the key episodes of his return, the temptations, the Sermon, and the murder. Through all these the highly serious theme of true martyrdom could be traced by means of the changing reactions of the Chorus of women, witnessing Becket's last days and gradually coming to discern God's purpose in willing the Archbishop's death While the events might be interesting in themselves the problem was to find a dramatic link between them for it was, after all, a drama, not just a pageant that Eliot was writing. The Chorus, of course, provides the perfect link.

The Chorus has the longest part in the play after Becket himself, indicating the value Eliot attaches to it. At first the women of Canterbury seem to experience nothing except their own petty discomfort and a vague sense of foreboding. Their gradual awakening and realisation of Becket's purpose give the play a sense of inevitable and proper movement forward.

The women of Canterbury are initially bewildered and distressed, waiting for some event which they dimly realise will have a profound effect on their lives, but whose nature and purpose they cannot grasp. They evoke a picture of the land, lying bare and cold under the winter weather, which gives local colour to the play and also serves as a symbolic expression of their mental state.

By contrasting their opening speeches with their last one in Part II, the extent of their discovery and progress can be measured—a progress of imagery as well as of ideas. In the *Te Deum* they recognise that 'snow', 'rain', 'wind', and 'storm', 'all Thy creatures both the hunters and the hunted' praise God and display his glory. Their earlier fear of prowling, creeping, predatory nature has passed away. Their vision of the corrupted and darkened earth convulsing in terror is purged by the Archbishop's sacrifice. Finally they come to a proper acceptance of their humble lot, and to an awareness of the need for mercy, and of the boundless extent of God's compassion.

This change manifests their role as patient witnesses of Becket's own struggle. Yet while we realise the great gulf which separates the powerful churchman from 'the scrubbers and sweepers of Canterbury', we are moved by his compassion for their ignorance and his infinite patience with their petty concerns. In Part I the Second Priest shows irritation at their bewilderment:

You are foolish, immodest and babbling women . . .
You go on croaking like frogs in the treetops:
But frogs at least can be cooked and eaten.

There is a degree of truth in this. We know the blindness and obtuseness of the Chorus. Yet Becket takes a much more charitable view:

Let them be, in their exultation.
They speak better than they know, and beyond your understanding.

This makes them seem less foolish and insignificant.

They fear for the physical safety of the man they look to as their father and protector. They do not realise that the danger is to Becket's soul more than to his body. Yet the fear does establish a relationship, and a starting point for their spiritual education. Thus the Chorus becomes real people, not just a piece of dramatic machinery. We are able to see events through their eyes as well as through Becket's: We share their gradual awakening in Part II. They are Eliot's means of focusing and directing the attention of the audience to the moral development of the play.

This is best illustrated by the martyrdom itself. The audience probably shares the bewilderment of the Chorus. Is it right that the father and protector of the poor should voluntarily seek his death, that he should abandon them? Why does he not go back to France where he will be safe, leaving them to their mundane existence, 'living and partly living'? What good can come of the shedding of his blood?

In Part I the Chorus asks these questions. The women feel imposed upon: 'do you realise what you ask, do you realise what it means / To the small folk drawn into the pattern of fate . . .?'

Their questions are those that we, the audience, would ask. Hence when they are gradually drawn towards understanding, we are drawn with them. There is a great spiritual leap forward between their speech 'Clear the air, clean the sky . . .' and the final *Te Deum*. Being forced to witness Becket's death in the light of the sermon he has preached on martyrdom, the message of his murder has finally come home. And we share it with them. When the play ends the Chorus has achieved a new and triumphant sense of understanding; 'wherever a martyr has given his blood for the blood of Christ, There is holy ground, and the sanctity shall not depart from it. . . .' The women acknowledge themselves as 'the types of common man', and are able to see the value and dignity of their common-ness. Hence, while their imagery does not change in subject matter, it changes in tone. Now they can accept the pattern of the seasons, the processes of nature, the evil in life as well as the good.

Eliot said that 'a poet writing for the first time for the stage, is much more at home in choral verse than in dramatic dialogue. . . . The use of the Chorus strengthened the power and concealed the defects of my theatrical technique.'* The strength of the writing in the part of the Chorus in *Murder in the Cathedral* bears witness to the truth of this assessment. Its colourful imagery is easy for the audience to grasp and sympathise with, centring on the land, houses and the unchanging daily lives of poor people. Within twenty-five lines of the play's opening we are reminded of harvest, winter fireside, floods, trade. Such things give a solid foundation to a play which is otherwise rather abstract in its themes.

The rhythms of the women's speech give vitality to the work. Their patterns of speech are varied from the enormously lengthened lines of their nausea and disgust, when they feel polluted by the murder, to the short lines of their repetitive rehearsals of the daily cycle of life.

The Chorus is at the centre of the play. Without the women of Canterbury to act as mediators between audience and action much of the moral point would be weakened. Upon the basically Greek form of dramatic structure which the Chorus implies, Eliot is able to build an intricate web of image and inward action. E. Martin Browne, the play's first producer, called the Chorus 'the most important single factor in the play's success', and it is impossible to disagree.

Examine the nature and function of the prose passages in Murder in the Cathedral

---

Plan

Introduction: two prose episodes in verse play—the Sermon, and the Knight's defence of the murder. Eliot's discussion of prose in verse drama in *Poetry and Drama* very relevant. He said (i) use prose sparingly; (ii) it creates a 'jolt'; (iii) hence reserve it for special effects.

Main body: Sermon—prose appropriate since sermons *should* be prose. Breaks up play into two halves. Language, style, rhythm all create contrast and provide 'still centre' in which message is underlined. The rhythms and language are biblical.

The Knights—deliberately 'modern' sound creates jolt to audience complacency; drags figures from history into twentieth century, thus making audience identify with problem; provides acid humour and variety; skilful use of rhetoric and debate technique.

*In *Poetry and Drama*, Faber & Faber, London, 1951, p.25.

Conclusions: two very different purposes served; one sanctifies, one
burlesques ideas; Becket made more dignified, Knights more banal;
both episodes make contrast with verse and lend it more intensity.

Essay
There are two prose episodes in *Murder in the Cathedral*: the Archbishop's Sermon (which comes exactly halfway through the play and
marks a major turning-point in the spiritual atmosphere) and the self-
defence of the Knights in Part II, after they have murdered Thomas.
This comes as a shocking anti-climax, calculated to jolt the audience
from complacency, and to thrust the play out of its medieval setting
into the context of our own lives and responses.

Clearly, two episodes with such different intentions will be markedly
dissimilar in language, rhythm, tone and impact. Both break the flow
of the verse, though the Sermon is much less disturbing than the Knights'
episode.

Becket's sermon provides a still centre during the action. Following
his crisis of conscience with the four tempters, its purpose is to clarify
the progress in his mind which has occurred through his victory over
temptation. The Knights' prose passage is a false summing-up, a
deliberate misstatement of a spiritual problem in secular terms. Whilst
we sympathise and agree with the one, we reject the other argument.

In *Poetry and Drama* Eliot gave his views on the mixture of prose and
verse in a play. Verse must justify itself as the basic medium of expression. It must be capable of covering all the events which take place
without appearing forced or unnatural; 'no play should be written in
verse for which prose is dramatically adequate'. The audience should
be unaware that the author is trying to manipulate their responses by
the medium itself. Style, rhythm and language must be natural to the
context in which they occur. Hence a mixture of prose and verse will
usually be undesirable, as the ear will be jolted from the rhythms of the
one to the other.

There may be occasions, however, when such a 'jolt' is desirable. The
two prose episodes in *Murder in the Cathedral* fulfil the dramatist's own
criteria for appropriateness and for effectiveness. Eliot maintained that
'the two prose episodes in *Murder in the Cathedral* could not have been
written in verse'. On the one hand a sermon in verse would be 'too unusual an experience for even the most regular church-goer', while the
Knights' platform prose was deliberately intended as a shock, which
verse would not have achieved.

The sermon is appropriate to this play for several reasons. We asso-
ciate this prose form particularly with the priest's teaching function in
church. Becket is a priest, he is in his own church, and he has an urgent
message to teach us. Historically we know that Becket preached to his

people on Christmas morning in 1170, just before he went to his death. Hence the factual justification is there. Eliot even sticks to the precise text Becket used. In dramatic terms the author is eager to make sure that the audience grasps the full significance of the temptations they have just seen Becket undergo, and the sermon on martyrdom allows him to drive the message home. The stage is cleared of all other actors, there are no distractions, our full attention is directed towards this man, who, knowing he is about to allow himself to be put to death, wishes to explain why he has made this choice.

At this natural pause in the action, we are given a summary of Part I and offered insight into the nature of Becket's actions in Part II.

Though the prose sermon may be something of a surprise, Eliot is careful to use biblical language and rhythms which will not disrupt the serious mood he has achieved in Part I. The language used for sermons has its own conventions with which most people are familiar. Hence the sermon is moulded into the texture and meaning of the surrounding verse. Standard forms of address like 'beloved' and 'brethren', the use of rhetorical questions, and reference to the Bible are all appropriately used.

The distance which a sermon puts between audience and speaker serves to create a pause in which we can weigh up the action so far, and its implications for Becket. He invites our attention through exhortations such as 'meditate', 'reflect', 'consider'. The long sentences with their colons and semi-colons create clauses which modify, expand and elaborate the ideas put forward. Repetition of key words such as 'mourn', 'rejoice', 'martyrdom' underlines the point of his argument.

These stylistic devices help the sermon to justify its place at the centre of the play. Though this is prose it has its own dignity, rhythm and style, and each of these supports the function of quiet reflection. The main point is that 'A Christian martyrdom is never an accident . . . still less . . . the effect of a man's will to become a saint . . .' In Part I Becket did not entirely grasp this, until after the fourth temptation. He had been inclined to seek his own death, perhaps for selfish reasons. Sharing his discovery during this quiet period of reflection helps the audience to a deeper sympathy and understanding.

The Knights' prose passage has precisely the opposite effect. It occurs just after the murder, when the sympathy of the audience for Becket is at its most intense, when the feelings of spectators and Chorus are over-wrought, and when, dramatically, we expect anything except a break into modern prose. It comes as a real shock when Fitz Urse moves to the front of the stage and begins 'We beg you to give us your attention for a few moments. . . .' This, it must be remembered, follows immediately from the cry of the Chorus, 'Clear the air, clean the stone, wash the wind. . . .' We are wrenched from the most intense emotional poetry to the most flat, banal prose, from moral crisis to specious explanation, from foul murder to bland board meeting, from 1170 to the present day.

The First Knight uses all the clichés of the chairman of a second-rate political gathering—'your sympathies are all with the underdog' . . . 'I am a man of action and not words'. He appeals to the lowest common ·denominator in our sympathy, whereas Becket in his Sermon drew us towards higher things. Likewise, as Becket's measured and dignified prose helped us to respect him, the platitudes of Fitz Urse and his colleagues tend to expose them as insensitive and limited men. Their inappropriate modernity makes them almost comic.

The sense of being present at a public debate is augmented by the Third Knight. He wants to appear close to the audience, to appeal to this common bond, so he makes himself sound ordinary and almost apologetic; 'we seemed a bit rowdy', 'I'm awfully sorry', 'a pretty stiff job', 'we are not getting a penny out of this'. Fitz Urse introduces him as 'my neighbour in the country', and de Traci does sound like a rather foolish country squire, with his exaggerated and quite false sense of fair play and decency. Because we know it is the murder of the Archbishop he is describing, we can see the more clearly how desperately inappropriate his language and sentiments really are. Yet he has a kind of insidious skill. He manages to make the deed sound less terrible than it was. Like many politicians he is dangerous because he can twist things to his own purpose.

The Second Knight is less bluff, more controlled in his language and style. His sentences are more complex and his vocabulary more polished. While his points of reference appeal to the ordinary sentiments of the audience he does not play down to them. He appeals to our sense of order, reason and fair play. One of his tactics is to admit that Becket was talented and useful. But he accuses the Archbishop of pride, therefore he had to be got rid of. And he attempts to make the audience identify with him: 'We have served your interests; we merit your applause. . . .' Then comes the sting in the tail of his argument: 'if there is any guilt . . . you must share it with us'. Clearly this man is a skilful speaker, able to twist notions like 'justice, service', 'merit', to his purpose. We have just witnessed a murder, a martyrdom, and now he would have us believe it was 'emotional clap-trap'.

What Eliot achieves by this speech is a reinforcement of our admiration for Becket. We *must* react against the Knight's clever but devious arguments. Set against the pure prose of Becket his words ring false, and by contrast with the fervour of the Chorus he is a cold fish indeed.

As the Fourth Tempter is the most subtle, so is the Fourth Knight the most dangerous. So completely does he seek to reverse logic and common sense that he would have us believe that Becket committed suicide. But unless we are very careful he may succeed, for the case he puts against Thomas is based on fact. His ability to twist and misrepresent the facts marks him as a master of words, though it is a debasement of language to use it in this way.

The First Knight draws us back towards the main action of the play by a gesture which is almost comic. He appeals to the listeners 'not to loiter in groups at street corners, and do nothing that might provoke any public outbreak'. This is a reminder of how timeless are the techniques of the dictator and the bureaucrat. The Knights have outraged public order. Now they fear that their own anarchy may be turned back upon themselves. In its utterly hackneyed rhythms and its cheap appeal to spurious authority this speech brings the prose episode to an appropriate climax.

Eliot then quickly reasserts the proper dignity of the play with the First Priest's lament for Becket, couched in measured verse, which contrasts most tellingly with the tinny prose of the Knights.

Both prose episodes in the play, then, have a vital function. Though they disrupt the flow of the verse, they do so for very different purposes, and they achieve their objectives by contrasting technical means. The Sermon employs biblical language and cadences to establish the proper decorum of pulpit oratory, and gives Becket a chance to share with us his spiritual discovery upon which the action of Part II will be based. Both structurally and ideologically the Sermon marks the turning-point of the drama.

In the Knights' prose we are dragged for a moment into the twentieth-century world of debate and argument contrived for partisan purposes. The resultant sense of shock awakens the audience to a heightened awareness of the effects of Becket's death.

Hence the use of prose in *Murder in the Cathedral* is consistent with Eliot's own ideas as he states them in *Poetry and Drama*. His practice has a subtlety and effectiveness which may surprise those who know him only as a poet. Without the prose episodes the play would be less varied and less rich, while the verse itself would suffer for lack of contrast with the rhythms of the prose.

Some further specimen questions

Questions on the characters

(1) Analyse the methods by which Eliot gives life and credibility to the character of Becket.

(2) To what extent and with what effect are the characters of the Knights, the Priests and the Tempters made individual?

(3) How far is Eliot's scope for individual characterisation limited by the kind of play he is writing in *Murder in the Cathedral*?

Questions on the themes

(1) Discuss the theme of martyrdom as Eliot presents it in *Murder in the Cathedral*.

(2) Discuss the nature of the temptations Becket has to undergo, and show how each fits into the overall pattern of the play.

(3) Eliot said of *Murder in the Cathedral*, 'I wanted to bring home to the audience the contemporary relevance of the situation'. By what means does he seek to achieve this aim, and how successful do you think he is?

Questions on the structure

(1) Consider the relationship between the structure of *Murder in the Cathedral* and that of (a) Greek drama, *and* (b) the pageant play.

(2) 'In the first act the strife is with shadows, in the second there is no strife at all.' (Helen Gardner) Discuss this view.

(3) 'The structure of the play is more dependent upon the growing moral awareness of the Chorus than upon the facts of the historical situation'. Discuss.

Questions on the language and poetry

(1) Analyse Eliot's use of language in creating the roles of the Priests and the Knights.

(2) Write a précis of any one of the speeches of the Chorus, to show that you fully understand its meaning. Then discuss the imagery of the speech.

(3) Examine the range and variety of the metre and rhythms in *Murder in the Cathedral*.

Part 5

Suggestions for further reading

The text

The text of *Murder in the Cathedral* has undergone various transmutations as the work has been adapted from the chapter house at Canterbury to the professional stage, and then again when it became a film. It is instructive to compare and contrast these differing versions. For examination purposes, however, you should make certain that you have the fourth or any subsequent edition. Eliot's works are published by Faber and Faber, London.

Criticism

ELIOT, T.S.: *Murder in the Cathedral*, Faber Educational Editions, Faber and Faber, London, 1965. This has an excellent introduction and notes by Nevill Coghill.

MASON, W.H.: *Murder in the Cathedral*, Notes on English Literature series, Blackwell, Oxford, 1962. There are excellent notes in this volume also.

GARDNER, HELEN: *The Art of T.S. Eliot*, Cresset Press, London, 1949.

ELIOT, T.S.: *Poetry and Drama*, Faber and Faber, London, 1950.

ELIOT, T.S.: *A Dialogue on Dramatic Poetry*, Faber and Faber, London, 1928. These two volumes give Eliot's own views on the play and on verse drama in general.

BROWNE, E. MARTIN: *The Making of T.S. Eliot's Plays*, Cambridge University Press, Cambridge, 1969. This book discusses the origins of the play and the process of adapting it for new theatres and productions.

BRAYBROOKE, N. (ED.): *T.S. Eliot, A Symposium for his Seventieth Birthday*, Hart-Davis, London, 1958. Robert Speaight, who first played the part of Becket, and George Hoellering, who directed the film, give their views on *Murder in the Cathedral*.

SMITH, GROVER: *T.S. Eliot's Poetry and Plays*, University of Chicago Press, Chicago, 1956. There are many books about Eliot's poetry; this is among the best of them, giving good coverage of the plays as well as the poetry.

The author of these notes

TONY BAREHAM is Senior Lecturer in English Studies at the New University of Ulster. Formerly Open Scholar at Lincoln College, Oxford, Dr Bareham earlier taught at the University of Rhodesia and the University of York. He has written a critical study of George Crabbe, and is co-author of the standard bibliography of the same poet. He has published various articles. His most recent work has been as contributing editor to a volume of essays on Anthony Trollope and as compiler of the 'Casebook' collection of criticism of Trollope. Dr Bareham also wrote the volume on Robert Bolt's *A Man For All Seasons* in the York Notes series.

York Notes: list of titles

CHINUA ACHEBE
A Man of the People
Arrow of God
Things Fall Apart

EDWARD ALBEE
Who's Afraid of Virginia Woolf?

ELECHI AMADI
The Concubine

ANONYMOUS
Beowulf
Everyman

JOHN ARDEN
Serjeant Musgrave's Dance

AYI KWEI ARMAH
The Beautyful Ones Are Not Yet Born

W. H. AUDEN
Selected Poems

JANE AUSTEN
Emma
Mansfield Park
Northanger Abbey
Persuasion
Pride and Prejudice
Sense and Sensibility

HONORÉ DE BALZAC
Le Père Goriot

SAMUEL BECKETT
Waiting for Godot

SAUL BELLOW
Henderson, The Rain King

ARNOLD BENNETT
Anna of the Five Towns

WILLIAM BLAKE
Songs of Innocence, Songs of Experience

ROBERT BOLT
A Man For All Seasons

ANNE BRONTË
The Tenant of Wildfell Hall

CHARLOTTE BRONTË
Jane Eyre

EMILY BRONTË
Wuthering Heights

ROBERT BROWNING
Men and Women

JOHN BUCHAN
The Thirty-Nine Steps

JOHN BUNYAN
The Pilgrim's Progress

BYRON
Selected Poems

ALBERT CAMUS
L'Etranger (The Outsider)

GEOFFREY CHAUCER
Prologue to the Canterbury Tales
The Franklin's Tale
The Knight's Tale
The Merchant's Tale
The Miller's Tale
The Nun's Priest's Tale
The Pardoner's Tale
The Wife of Bath's Tale
Troilus and Criseyde

ANTON CHEKHOV
The Cherry Orchard

SAMUEL TAYLOR COLERIDGE
Selected Poems

WILKIE COLLINS
The Moonstone
The Woman in White

SIR ARTHUR CONAN DOYLE
The Hound of the Baskervilles

WILLIAM CONGREVE
The Way of the World

JOSEPH CONRAD
Heart of Darkness
Lord Jim
Nostromo
The Secret Agent
Victory
Youth and *Typhoon*

STEPHEN CRANE
The Red Badge of Courage

BRUCE DAWE
Selected Poems

WALTER DE LA MARE
Selected Poems

DANIEL DEFOE
A Journal of the Plague Year
Moll Flanders
Robinson Crusoe

CHARLES DICKENS
A Tale of Two Cities
Bleak House
David Copperfield
Great Expectations
Hard Times
Little Dorrit
Nicholas Nickleby
Oliver Twist
Our Mutual Friend
The Pickwick Papers

EMILY DICKINSON
Selected Poems

JOHN DONNE
Selected Poems

THEODORE DREISER
Sister Carrie

GEORGE ELIOT
Adam Bede
Middlemarch
Silas Marner
The Mill on the Floss

T. S. ELIOT
Four Quartets
Murder in the Cathedral
Selected Poems
The Cocktail Party
The Waste Land

J. G. FARRELL
The Siege of Krishnapur

GEORGE FARQUHAR
The Beaux Stratagem

WILLIAM FAULKNER
Absalom, Absalom!
As I Lay Dying
Go Down, Moses
The Sound and the Fury

HENRY FIELDING
Joseph Andrews
Tom Jones

F. SCOTT FITZGERALD
Tender is the Night
The Great Gatsby

E. M. FORSTER
A Passage to India
Howards End

ATHOL FUGARD
Selected Plays

JOHN GALSWORTHY
Strife

MRS GASKELL
North and South

WILLIAM GOLDING
Lord of the Flies
The Inheritors
The Spire

OLIVER GOLDSMITH
She Stoops to Conquer
The Vicar of Wakefield

ROBERT GRAVES
Goodbye to All That

GRAHAM GREENE
Brighton Rock
The Heart of the Matter
The Power and the Glory

THOMAS HARDY
Far from the Madding Crowd
Jude the Obscure
Selected Poems
Tess of the D'Urbervilles
The Mayor of Casterbridge
The Return of the Native
The Trumpet Major
The Woodlanders
Under the Greenwood Tree

L. P. HARTLEY
The Go-Between
The Shrimp and the Anemone

NATHANIEL HAWTHORNE
The Scarlet Letter

SEAMUS HEANEY
Selected Poems

ERNEST HEMINGWAY
A Farewell to Arms
For Whom the Bell Tolls
The African Stories
The Old Man and the Sea

GEORGE HERBERT
Selected Poems

HERMANN HESSE
Steppenwolf

BARRY HINES
Kes

HOMER
The Iliad

ANTHONY HOPE
The Prisoner of Zenda

GERARD MANLEY HOPKINS
Selected Poems

WILLIAM DEAN HOWELLS
The Rise of Silas Lapham

RICHARD HUGHES
A High Wind in Jamaica

THOMAS HUGHES
Tom Brown's Schooldays

ALDOUS HUXLEY
Brave New World

HENRIK IBSEN
A Doll's House
Ghosts
Hedda Gabler

HENRY JAMES
Daisy Miller
The Europeans
The Portrait of a Lady
The Turn of the Screw
Washington Square

SAMUEL JOHNSON
Rasselas

BEN JONSON
The Alchemist
Volpone

JAMES JOYCE
A Portrait of the Artist as a Young Man
Dubliners

JOHN KEATS
Selected Poems

RUDYARD KIPLING
Kim

D. H. LAWRENCE
Sons and Lovers
The Rainbow
Women in Love

CAMARA LAYE
L'Enfant Noir

HARPER LEE
To Kill a Mocking-Bird

LAURIE LEE
Cider with Rosie

THOMAS MANN
Tonio Kröger

CHRISTOPHER MARLOWE
Doctor Faustus
Edward II

ANDREW MARVELL
Selected Poems

W. SOMERSET MAUGHAM
Of Human Bondage
Selected Short Stories

J. MEADE FALKNER
Moonfleet

HERMAN MELVILLE
Billy Budd
Moby Dick

THOMAS MIDDLETON
Women Beware Women

THOMAS MIDDLETON and WILLIAM ROWLEY
The Changeling

ARTHUR MILLER
Death of a Salesman
The Crucible

JOHN MILTON
Paradise Lost I & II
Paradise Lost IV & IX
Selected Poems

V. S. NAIPAUL
A House for Mr Biswas

SEAN O'CASEY
Juno and the Paycock
The Shadow of a Gunman

GABRIEL OKARA
The Voice

EUGENE O'NEILL
Mourning Becomes Electra

GEORGE ORWELL
Animal Farm
Nineteen Eighty-four

JOHN OSBORNE
Look Back in Anger

WILFRED OWEN
Selected Poems

ALAN PATON
Cry, The Beloved Country

THOMAS LOVE PEACOCK
Nightmare Abbey and *Crotchet Castle*

HAROLD PINTER
The Birthday Party
The Caretaker

PLATO
The Republic

ALEXANDER POPE
Selected Poems

THOMAS PYNCHON
The Crying of Lot 49

SIR WALTER SCOTT
Ivanhoe
Quentin Durward
The Heart of Midlothian
Waverley

PETER SHAFFER
The Royal Hunt of the Sun

WILLIAM SHAKESPEARE
A Midsummer Night's Dream
Antony and Cleopatra
As You Like It
Coriolanus
Cymbeline
Hamlet
Henry IV Part I
Henry IV Part II
Henry V
Julius Caesar
King Lear
Love's Labour's Lost
Macbeth
Measure for Measure
Much Ado About Nothing
Othello
Richard II
Richard III
Romeo and Juliet
Sonnets
The Merchant of Venice
The Taming of the Shrew
The Tempest
The Winter's Tale
Troilus and Cressida
Twelfth Night
The Two Gentlemen of Verona

GEORGE BERNARD SHAW
Androcles and the Lion
Arms and the Man
Caesar and Cleopatra
Candida
Major Barbara
Pygmalion
Saint Joan
The Devil's Disciple

MARY SHELLEY
Frankenstein

PERCY BYSSHE SHELLEY
Selected Poems

RICHARD BRINSLEY SHERIDAN
The School for Scandal
The Rivals

WOLE SOYINKA
The Lion and the Jewel
The Road
Three Short Plays

EDMUND SPENSER
The Faerie Queene (Book I)

JOHN STEINBECK
Of Mice and Men
The Grapes of Wrath
The Pearl

LAURENCE STERNE
A Sentimental Journey
Tristram Shandy

ROBERT LOUIS STEVENSON
Kidnapped
Treasure Island
Dr Jekyll and Mr Hyde

TOM STOPPARD
Professional Foul
Rosencrantz and Guildenstern are Dead

JONATHAN SWIFT
Gulliver's Travels

JOHN MILLINGTON SYNGE
The Playboy of the Western World

TENNYSON
Selected Poems

W. M. THACKERAY
Vanity Fair

DYLAN THOMAS
Under Milk Wood

EDWARD THOMAS
Selected Poems

FLORA THOMPSON
Lark Rise to Candleford

J. R. R. TOLKIEN
The Hobbit
The Lord of the Rings

CYRIL TOURNEUR
The Revenger's Tragedy

ANTHONY TROLLOPE
Barchester Towers

MARK TWAIN
Huckleberry Finn
Tom Sawyer

VIRGIL
The Aeneid

VOLTAIRE
Candide

EVELYN WAUGH
Decline and Fall
A Handful of Dust

JOHN WEBSTER
The Duchess of Malfi
The White Devil

H. G. WELLS
The History of Mr Polly
The Invisible Man
The War of the Worlds

ARNOLD WESKER
Chips with Everything
Roots

PATRICK WHITE
Voss

OSCAR WILDE
The Importance of Being Earnest

TENNESSEE WILLIAMS
The Glass Menagerie

VIRGINIA WOOLF
To the Lighthouse

WILLIAM WORDSWORTH
Selected Poems

W. B. YEATS
Selected Poems